Topics in Autism

SIBLINGS of CHILDREN with AUTISM
A Guide for Families

Sandra L. Harris, Ph.D.

Michael Powers, Series Editor

WOODBINE HOUSE 1994

Published by Woodbine House, 6510 Bells Mill Road,
Bethesda, MD 20817, 800/843–7323.

Cover illustration & design: Liz Wolf

Library of Congress Cataloging-in-Publication Data

Harris, Sandra L.
  Siblings of children with autism : a guide for families / by Sandra
L. Harris.
    p. cm. — (Topics in autism)
  Includes bibliographical references and index.
  ISBN 0–933149–71–9 : $12.95
  1. Autistic children—Family relationships. I. Title.
II. Series.
RJ506.A9H27 1994   94–18177
649'.154—dc20   CIP

Manufactured in the United States of America

10 9 8 7 6 5 4 3

For Joseph Masling

Who knew I could before I did

Contents

Preface

For more than 20 years I have had the privilege of working with families which include a child with autism. They have invited me into their homes, shared their sorrows and their triumphs, and trusted me with their children. Those families and I have learned a great deal together. We have watched educational technology for children with autism grow increasingly sophisticated, and rejoiced together over some of the very impressive results of this intensive education. We have watched fads in treatment come and go, sometimes sharing a sense of sorrow that our field is still so imperfect that we are vulnerable to these passing fancies. Most importantly, we have marched together slowly and steadily, with each year showing more progress than the one before it.

As I have worked with these families, and grown older with them, I have had an opportunity to know the siblings as well as the parents. In recent years I have felt increasing concern that we do not always meet the needs of siblings in the family of a child with autism. Often we are so focused on the intensive educational needs of the child with autism that we tend to slide past the needs of the other children. But when I listen to the voices of these young people in sibling support groups, or in individual conversations, I am struck by the urgency of their needs. It was that awareness that led me to write this book for parents and professionals.

I hope this book will be useful to parents of children with autism in thinking about the needs of all of their family members. I hope it will also be helpful to the professionals who serve them. I have tried to address some of the compelling questions that parents raise with me in our conversations about their children. If you find the book useful perhaps you will write to me and let me know what about it was helpful. I will also be interested in your suggestions for additional topics, or your comments on topics where you disagree with me. I would like to make the next edition of this book even better than this one.

Although this book has only my name as author, many people have contributed to it. First, and most important, I wish to thank all of the families over the years who have honored me with a window into the life of their family. Three mothers in particular, Stephanie Baslie, Donna Icovino, and Monica O'Connor, wrote material which appears at the end of each chapter, reflecting a parent's perspective; other family contributors wished to remain anonymous. I very much appreciate their thoughtfulness and their help. I have carefully disguised the identity of every family member to protect his or her privacy. Remember as you read these vignettes that the children with autism vary widely in the severity of their disorder and degree of mental retardation. Susan Stokes, Irvin Shapell, and Michael Powers provided valuable editorial support for the book. It is a privilege to publish with Woodbine House.

My colleagues at the Douglass Developmental Disabilities Center, especially Jan Handleman, Maria Arnold, Rita Gordon, and Barbara Kristoff have been a source of support over the years, without them there would be no school. I also thank Jean L. Burton who was instrumental in launching the Douglass Developmental Disabilities Center, our on-campus school for children with autism. My colleagues at the Graduate School of Applied and Professional Psychology have provided the context for my life as a scholar. Han van den Blink helped me understand the importance of thinking about the individual's behavior within the family setting.

Finally, I want to thank my brother Jay E. Harris, who taught me from day one of my life what it means to grow up as the sister of a loving big brother.

Piscataway, NJ
Spring, 1994

1 | BROTHERS AND SISTERS: Getting Together and Getting Along

The McGuire Family

Bang! The screen door slammed. Thump, thump, thump! Small feet ran hard up the hallway stairs to the second floor. Thud! The bedroom door slammed shut. Shortly the sounds of loud music erased all traces of silence in the McGuire household. Sally McGuire sighed deeply and shook her head. Something was bothering 10–year-old Kevin. But it was harder and harder to know what the boy was thinking or feeling. He was getting increasingly moody. Sometimes he was still a little boy who liked to cuddle with her, but more often now he held his distance. Her little adolescent!

Sally had little time to be lost in reverie. Her younger son, Mitch, was tugging at her leg. "Want juice." Her face brightened. "Great talking, Mitch," said Sally as she moved to the refrigerator and found his favorite drink. Mitch was five years old this month, and a couple of years ago Sally despaired that he would ever speak. She and her husband, Tom, had gone from one specialist to another seeking an answer to the puzzle of their son's behavior. Finally, when he was nearly three years old they found a psychologist who understood Mitch. She had told the McGuires as gently as she could that Mitch had a developmental condition called Autis-

tic Disorder. He would require years of intensive education to reach his potential and would probably require some special services all of his life.

Sally and Tom, although dismayed about Mitch's diagnosis, were relieved finally to know what was happening to him, and grateful to know how to help him. Soon they enrolled Mitch in a good preschool class and were immersed in home programming which required them to become very skillful teachers for Mitch. Their hard, time-consuming work was paying off in important changes in his behavior. He spoke now, and had pretty much stopped his tantrums. He also seemed happier than they had ever known him.

The front doorbell rang. It was the McGuires' next door neighbor, Rosemary Vandenbeck, who had known the McGuires for nearly ten years and had been a wonderful source of support with Mitch. Rosemary looked concerned. "Is Kevin around?" Sally said he was in his room. Rosemary went on to share with Sally what she had overheard in her backyard just a few minutes before Kevin had gone pounding up the stairs.

Kevin had been sitting on the back steps talking with Rosemary's boy Jon. Their words drifted through the open window to where Rosemary was seated at her computer. The word "autism" caught her ear and she paused for a minute to listen. Kevin was telling Jon that he had a secret thought about his brother, Mitch. Sometimes he wished Mitch wasn't his brother, but that Jon was. His parents thought every little thing Mitch did was great, but they never paid any attention to what Kevin did. Sometimes he wondered if they really loved him as much as they loved Mitch. He knew Mitch had autism, but that didn't mean he should be able to get away

*with anything he wanted. Kevin felt like he had to be extra
good at everything to make up for what Mitch could not do.
None of it was fair!*

*As she heard this story from Rosemary, Sally felt an ache
for Kevin, who had been bearing all his pain without saying a
word. And then she felt alarm because she had not understood Kevin well enough to see how bothered he was. Something had to be done, but how could she reach a son who
seemed so remote?*

Introduction

Kevin McGuire's feelings about his brother Mitch are not
unusual. Many children in his situation have had times when
they felt their parents loved them less than they did another
child who had autism. Neither is his difficulty sharing his feelings with his parents unusual. It is not easy for many children
to tell their parents their concerns about their brother or sister with autism.

Several things may be contributing to Kevin's silence.
These include his sense of shame about his jealousy, his frustration because his parents are often busy with Mitch and do
not seem to have much time for him, and his own beginning
entry to adolescence, with a normal, gradual withdrawal from
the world of the family to the world of peers. Each of these factors could, and probably did, contribute to Kevin's silence.

Do problems like those faced by the McGuire family mean
the barriers between parents and children are too high for
good communication about a brother or sister with autism?
Thankfully, they do not. Although the quality of family communication varies across time and across the developmental

stages of a child's life, parents and children need not lose touch with one another about the important things in their lives. But good communication does not always come easily, and sometimes requires extra effort from everyone in the family.

This chapter summarizes some of what social scientists know about the relationships between normally developing siblings. It then examines the effect on these normal patterns of behavior when one of the children in the family has autism or a similar disorder. This chapter will help you understand the many different healthy ways children can learn to get along with each other. Chapter 2 describes what kind of information you might share with your child about autism, and how a child's need for information changes with age. Chapter 3 takes a look at what you can do to increase family communication. Chapter 4 examines some of the specific things you can do to help your children cope with the special needs of their brother or sister with autism. I will consider how the entire family can strike a healthy balance between inclusion and separateness, so that the needs of each family member are met as well as possible. Chapter 5 focuses on helping children become playmates for a sibling with autism. This chapter includes suggestions for teaching play skills to your children.

I have written this book from the perspective of a family which consists of two parents and their biological children. However, I understand that many other healthy combinations are possible in families including adopted children, stepchildren, and foster children, and in single parent families.

Having worked with the many varied family constellations, I believe that most of the information I am offering will be useful for every family regardless of its structure. However, the single parent who must raise a child with autism without a supportive partner, or the blended family where a stepparent must learn to become part of an established family, and take on responsibilities for a child with autism, encounter special demands. For example, a normally developing stepchild not only has to learn to accept a new stepparent, but is cast into the role of sibling of a child with autism. Both the stepparent and stepchild may feel overwhelmed by these new roles.

Similarly, when the sibling relationship is based not on biology, but on adoption, family members will have questions of adoption to deal with, as well as the difficulties created by one child's autism. Some families elect to adopt a child with autism, and others discover the disability after the adoption is complete. In either case, the fact of adoption is an additional variable that can affect the family (Brodzinsky & Schechter, 1990).

Any one of these challenges, being a single parent, stepparent, foster parent, or adoptive parent, places special demands on a person. When the needs of a child with autism are added to these basic family demands, some families may find they would benefit from professional consultations to address the many issues they face. This might be with a psychologist, psychiatrist, social worker, family therapist, or a religious advisor who has had training in pastoral counseling. It helps if this professional has worked with people with autism. One way to find such a person may be through your local autism society chapter; other families who have had a good therapy experience, a child's teacher, or a pediatrician may also be good referral sources. See Table 1 for a list of some of the professionals who provide support services for families and their children with autism. As discussed in Chapter 4, it is impor-

TABLE 1
Professionals Who May Be Able to Help

Clinical Psychologist Has a doctorate in psychology and is licensed or certified by state. Clinical psychologists study human behavior and mental processes with the goal of reducing suffering and increasing self-understanding and healthy functioning. May work in public agency or private practice. Does behavioral intervention with child, parent training, diagnosis, and individual, marital, or family therapy. Provides consultation for finding community resources.

Family Therapist May be a social worker, psychologist, psychiatrist, pastoral counselor, or marriage and family therapist who specializes in work with families.

Neurologist Has an MD degree with specialized training in brain function. Consultation regarding diagnosis, medication, and community resources.

Psychiatrist Has an MD degree with special training in psychiatry. Because of their medical training psychiatrists have specialized, in-depth understanding of the biological factors underlying human behavior and have the expertise to prescribe medication and other medical treatments. Provides consultation regarding diagnosis, medication, and community resources. May do individual, marital, or family therapy.

School Psychologist Has a master's degree or doctorate in school psychology. Licensed or certified by the state. May work in schools, public agencies, or private practice. Provides consultation regarding diagnosis, behavioral intervention for child, parent training, resources in community, and individual, marital, or family therapy.

Special Education Teacher Has a bachelor's or master's degree in education. Licensed by state. Works in school setting. Provides consultation regarding behavioral intervention with child, parent training, and resources in community.

tant to ask for help from family or professional helpers when you encounter tough problems in raising your child with autism.

Another sometimes overlooked factor that may make life more difficult for the family of a child with autism is the increased frequency with which siblings suffer from disorders related to autism. We know, for example, that siblings of children with autism have a greater risk for problems of general intelligence, reading, and language (Folstein & Rutter, 1987). No one is exactly sure why these difficulties are more common in siblings, but the problems seem to have a genetic link with autism. For example, in 1981 researchers tested the siblings of 41 children with autism and found that 15 had mental retardation (August, Stewart, & Tsai, 1981). Similarly, in an older study, a family history of reading or language disabilities was reported in 5 of 19 families of children with autism (Bartak, Rutter, & Cox, 1975).

One family I knew had a child with autism, another with a learning disability, and a third who was developing without any evident problems. These parents spent a great deal of time shuttling back and forth from one special program to another, and from one doctor's office to the next. Trying to balance their family needs eventually led them into marital therapy in an effort to bring order to the chaos.

Fortunately, most siblings of children with autism do not have learning problems, and when they do, they are not as challenged as the child with autism. However, when learning problems are present, siblings will need considerable help if they are to meet their potential. Under these circumstances, you will have your hands full meeting the special needs of two or more children and helping them develop their sibling relationship as well.

Siblings Across a Lifetime

Brothers and sisters are not just for childhood. These relationships, at least in their formal sense, continue across our lifetime. For many adults, the person who has known us longest and best is our sibling. However, the quality of sibling relationships varies widely, and some of us are blessed with a sense of intimacy in our interactions with our brother or sister, while others of us hardly know this person with whom we share a profound biological bond. Although we choose our friendships, our brothers and sisters are imposed on us, and even if we are emotionally distanced from them, they remain part of the fabric of our lives.

In thinking about how your children get along with each other, it is helpful to understand that there are a variety of styles of sibling relationships which are "normal." You should also know that sibling relationships change as children grow up. There is no single prescription for how brothers and sisters should get along.

The Sibling Bond

In 1982, psychologists Stephen Bank and Michael Kahn studied the sibling bond through extensive interviews of several hundred siblings of different ages, gender, and social circumstances. They point to a process of "access" as one of the factors that creates an emotional bond between children. High access, with strong sibling bonds, is most likely to occur when children are close in age, of the same gender, and have shared many activities. Not surprisingly, low access with subsequent weaker bonds, often occurs when children are widely separated in age, have spent relatively little time together, and are of different gender. It is not essential that siblings share these qualities to form a strong bond, but they increase the likelihood of such a strength of connection. A strong bond does not always mean a happy bond. Bank and Kahn (1982) point out that a strong sibling bond can be warm and loving, but also can be negative and tension filled. The sense of connection between siblings can be a source of joy or of pain.

Early Childhood

The interaction between siblings changes as children grow up. A good relationship at age 5 will be different at age 15. Nonetheless, the foundation for connection is laid down in early childhood. Warmth and affection early in childhood lay the foundation for intimacy and caring later on.

One of the first things you might think about siblings in early childhood is the reaction of an older child to the birth of a baby brother or sister, and the experience of "sibling rivalry." Many things change when a baby is born. For example, the birth of a younger brother or sister means a change in your relationship with your other child. You can no longer devote all your energies to that child. That change in attention often produces at least temporary behavior problems for the older child including difficulties with toileting, withdrawal, aggressiveness, dependency, and anxiety (Dunn, 1992). However, in spite of their transient discomfort, most children adjust well to a new baby. The role of parents is crucial in this adjustment. How you talk to your child about the baby is important in how the two of them will get along (Dunn, 1992).

Children need support and reassurance that they are still loved, respected, and special, while they learn to live with the new little stranger in their lives. It is easy for adults to underestimate the impact on a child when a baby enters the family.

The process of change in sibling relationships continues year by year. One of the important transitions in the interactions of brothers and sisters happens when the younger child is between three and four years of age. By this age, children have skills that make them increasingly desirable companions for childhood play. These skills include complex language, motor abilities, and a social repertoire which make them attractive playmates for their older brother or sister. As a result, the older child begins to take an increasing interest in the younger (Dunn, 1992). By this age, the possibilities for both companionship and competition begin to emerge and the range of potential sibling interactions grows increasingly rich and complex. Young children who are closer together in age are likely to experience more quarrels and tension than are children four or more years apart (Buhrmester, 1992), but they are also likely to develop a closer emotional bond.

The overall quality of family life has an important impact on how siblings get along with one another. Parents who have a good marriage and effectively resolve difference between themselves are more likely to have children who can do the same. Similarly, parents who are effective care takers for their children are likely to have children who relate well to one another (Boer, Goedhart, & Treffers, 1992). Being an effective parent includes such qualities as conveying respect, warmth, and love, being consistent in one's expectations and rules, setting clear limits on children's inappropriate behaviors, and providing predictable but flexible childhood routines.

In families where there are serious parental problems, siblings can be an important source of support for one another (Jenkins, 1992), but these relationships cannot replace the love and wisdom of a competent parent. These findings highlight how important it is for parents to maintain a healthy marriage, not only for themselves, but for their children as well.

Middle Childhood and Adolescence

Changes in sibling interactions continue in middle childhood, from about 9 to 12 years of age. Judy Dunn (1992), an expert on sibling relationships, reports that during middle childhood there is an important change in how siblings get along. This is a time when the interactions between children become more equal and balanced. During early childhood most of the caretaking between siblings flows from the older to the younger child; however, when the younger sibling reaches 11 or 12 years of age, the older sibling does less nurturing, creating a more balanced relationship between the children.

In addition to the shift in caretaking, there is also a shift in dominance, with the younger child achieving a more equal footing with the older by about 12 years of age. This greater equity in caretaking and power may benefit both children. The younger child has reached an age of increased independence, and the older child is no longer responsible for looking after the younger, and may have more freedom to pursue adolescent goals (Buhrmester, 1992). Although many siblings report a relatively high level of conflict with their brother or sister during preadolescence and early adolescence, by middle to late adolescence there is a marked decline in this tension (Buhrmester, 1992).

During early and middle childhood and preadolescence, parents and siblings are the most important sources of emotional support and sharing. Parents play the central support role for children until sixth or seventh grade. They help their children solve problems, comfort their distress, and share a range of activities and interests. However, after that age, family members decline in importance, as friends, and later romantic relationships, grow in meaning (Buhrmester, 1992). This does not mean that the family becomes unimportant, but there is a shift in the balance of relationships toward those outside of the home. This shift is part of the developmental process that enables children to become competent independent adults in Western culture.

Adulthood

Sibling relationships can remain important throughout our lives. With increasingly smaller family size, longer life spans, and a greater probability of divorce and remarriage, the sibling relationship may be more important today than it was 100 years ago (Bank & Kahn, 1982). Friendships may be lost in moves, marriages dissolve, and parents die, but the sibling relationship may endure through all of these transitions. In old age our brother or sister may remain the sole link with our past.

When a Brother or Sister Has Autism

What happens to the normal course of sibling relationships when one of the children has autism and is unable to respond in the usual fashion to the joy, the play, and to the rough and tumble of childhood? It is easy to imagine the frustration and disappointment an older sister feels when her younger sister shows no interest in playing childhood games. After a while she will probably give up trying to relate to her and focus her energy on other people. The sibling relationship may become one of sadness or indifference.

A school-aged child will be understandably angry when his brother with autism comes into his room and destroys a model airplane that the older boy has labored over for several days. Children of any age may begin to doubt their worth and importance when their parents seem preoccupied with their sibling with autism and appear to have no time for them. We saw a vivid example of this in the case of Kevin and Mitch McGuire. Kevin resented the time his parents spent with Mitch and wondered if they loved Mitch more than him.

Of course, these kinds of frustration are not unique to families where there is a child with autism. Most of us have been angry at our brother or sister, and there are few of us who never felt that our sibling was getting more parental attention than he or she deserved. So, it is important to recognize the difference between the normal frustration of childhood and the special impact of having a sibling with autism or a related developmental disability. Some of these differences are discussed later in this chapter.

You will find it reassuring to know that the research shows most children who have a sibling with autism learn to handle the experience, and show no major ill effects (e.g.,

McHale, Sloan, & Simeonsson, 1986). Nonetheless, there are special demands growing up in a household where one child has autism. Although some children learn to deal with these demands, others have greater difficulty. While serious behavior problems rarely arise when a child has a sibling with autism, brothers and sisters do have to grapple with the special demands imposed on them. If you understand these demands, you may be able to ease your child's burden. Ultimately, if things go better for your child, they will go better for you as well.

Older Sisters/Younger Brothers

Early research on siblings' experiences looked mainly at things such as birth order (first born, middle, or last), and age and gender of the child with a developmental disability and the normally developing siblings. For example, older sisters and younger brothers were sometimes found to be at greater risk for emotional problems than other children (Seligman & Darling, 1989). However, this relationship between age and gender is complicated, not well understood, and does not always occur. Furthermore, even if we knew that these two groups of children were at greater risk for difficulties, we would still not know much about what specific emotional or behavior problems were bothering them. Although the early research highlighted some potential trouble spots, it did not tell us much about what was actually going on in families that made some children very unhappy, while in other families children coped well.

More recently researchers have looked in greater detail at the experience of growing up with a brother or sister who is developmentally disabled. For example, psychologist Susan

McHale and her colleagues found that children between the ages of 6 and 15 had mostly positive things to say about their brother or sister, regardless of whether the sibling had autism, mental retardation, or was developing normally (McHale, Sloan, & Simeonsson, 1986). However, these researchers caution that siblings of children with handicapping conditions gave varied responses. Some children had very positive things to say about their experiences with a brother or sister with autism or mental retardation, and others were quite negative. The siblings in the negative group often said they were worried about the future of the child with a handicap, and they believed their parents favored that child. By contrast, children who viewed both parents and peers as responding positively to the child's disability, and who had a good factual understanding of the disability tended to have a more positive relationship with their brother or sister.

Another team of researchers compared siblings of children with autism to siblings of children with Down syndrome and of normally developing children (Rodrique, Geffken, & Morgan, 1993). They found that the parents of the children with autism reported more concerns about what psychologists call internalizing and externalizing problems. Internalizing symptoms are those we experience inwardly like depression and anxiety, while externalizing symptoms are turned outside of ourselves in behaviors like aggression, defiance, or running away. Although both of these kinds of problems were more frequent in the children who had siblings with autism, the young people as a group still fell within the normal range of behavior. In addition, on the positive side, the siblings of the children with autism did not differ from the other two groups in their self-esteem. The findings of more emotional and behavior problems in the siblings of children with autism support the idea that it is harder to be the sibling of a child with autism than of a child with another disability, and heighten the importance for parents of being alert to children's struggles.

Both of these research studies are consistent with my own experiences working with siblings across the age spectrum. It appears that most children are resilient to the impact of their brother's or sister's special needs. Nonetheless, there are challenges involved in growing up in a family where a sibling has autism. The purpose of this book is to help the reader understand these potential issues and be able to minimize their impact.

Special Demands

Researchers Milton Seligman and Rosalyn Darling (1989) point to several areas where siblings of children with autism may need help learning to cope. One of these areas is the need for information. Parents may not communicate openly or effectively to children about the nature of autism. The lack of information leaves a big space in the child's mind to be filled by misinformation, fears, and fantasies. They will create their own explanations, worry needlessly about whether they harmed their sibling, or imagine a future life for themselves or their sibling far more bleak than reality.

Young children in particular have a difficult time distinguishing wish and reality, and may become very confused about their sibling's disability. Although they hear the word "autism," they may not understand what it means. They may, for example, be afraid that they caused the autism by some misbehavior or angry thought, or that they can "catch" autism as they would a cold. To compound matters, as noted earlier in the case of Kevin and Mitch McGuire, children may be afraid to ask questions or raise problems because they do not wish to upset their parents or because they are ashamed of their own feelings of anger, jealousy, or resentment. Children growing up under these conditions may learn to conceal feelings, deny their emotions to themselves, and develop an inconsistency between feelings and actions. Such maladaptive behaviors can intrude on their adult capacity for intimacy and form a barrier to relationships with other people. Fortunately, it is usually possible for parents to recognize and address these childhood concerns.

A lack of understanding about autism can also diminish a child's feeling of being a unique and special person, entitled to lead a separate life. Some children may overly identify with the sibling and feel responsible for the child's disability (Seligman & Darling, 1989). A lack of information may make it difficult for the normally developing child to have a clear sense of himself as a unique person, and not as an extension of his brother. For example, a boy may be reluctant to go away to summer camp because his younger brother with autism cannot go as well. It may be hard for him to understand that he can have a separate, happy life apart from his brother. Such a pattern, if sustained over time, may result in an adult who cannot lay claim to a basic right to exist as a special, unique person. In order to establish healthy adult relationships, we need to experience the legitimacy of our own needs as well as those of the other person. Again, a perceptive parent can often recognize the seeds of such a problem.

Chapter 2 will discuss what kinds of things you will want to tell your child about autism, and how you can convey that information according to the age of your child. This information may give your child a realistic sense of his sibling's special needs and why there are differences in how the two of them are treated.

Children with autism usually do not meet their siblings' expectations as playmates. As I noted earlier in this chapter, at the age of three or four years of age, normally developing children begin to be real companions to an older brother or sister. For example, he may be the "baby" in a pretend family or enjoy roughhousing in the backyard. By contrast, at that same age a younger sibling with autism may demonstrate a number of troubling autistic behaviors and be a difficult if not impossible playmate. The child with autism may destroy toys, be aggressive, or have severe tantrums when approached by a sibling. The consistent rejection experienced by the normally developing child may lead him to give up trying to play with his sibling. In Chapter 5, I will discuss how you can teach your children skills which may help them become playmates with their brother or sister with autism. This may help to strengthen the bond between your children.

Caretaking is another area that has been identified as a potential problem area for normally developing siblings (Seligman & Darling, 1989). Older children, especially older sisters of children with mental retardation, spend more time in caretaking roles than do other siblings (McHale & V. Harris, 1992). For example, a sibling may help her brother with autism dress in the morning or supervise his play while parents prepare dinner. The more even distribution of care giving that usually happens when a younger child reaches 11 or 12 years of age typically does not occur in families where the younger child has autism. As a result, the older child may have a more difficult time achieving her adolescent independence unless parents are especially sensitive to her needs. Parents must be alert to the danger of allowing their adolescent child to be too good a helper, thereby interfering with her social development.

These inequities of the caretaking relationship can affect younger siblings as well as older ones. For younger siblings the reversal of traditional roles can be especially perplexing. For example, a 9–year-old sister may find herself looking after a 13–year-old brother, in stark contrast to the typical age-appropriate roles she sees in other families. She may resent having to care for someone physically older and larger, be embarrassed to have her friends see her caring for him, and she may feel guilty about being younger and more competent than her big brother. In the normal course of events, older children care for younger ones, and children may be acutely aware of being different from their peers in this regard. The sense of being different can make a child feel angry, ashamed, embarrassed, sad, or defiant. She may avoid being with her brother, not want to have friends over to play when he is home, or perhaps join in when her friends tease him.

Helping take care of a sibling need not be harmful when carefully balanced with opportunities for other activities, but excessive burdens can harm the development of the child and a positive sibling bond. The normally developing sibling is not an auxiliary parent of the sibling with autism and should not be expected to assume major responsibilities for that child. On the other hand, every child should contribute to the welfare of the family. The challenge is to find age-appropriate ways for children to make these contributions. Chapter 4 discusses how you can communicate effectively with your children about responsibilities and privileges, and help your normally developing child understand that the greater attention you must sometimes pay to the child with autism does not reflect a difference in love for the children. The chapter also discusses distribution of family responsibilities and opportunities.

Most of us feel angry from time to time. It is not surprising that siblings of children with autism must struggle with this emotion. Anger can arise if siblings are given excessive responsibilities for the child with special needs, if they feel their social life is limited, if they lose parental attention, and if there is a drain of family resources (Seligman & Darling, 1989). In the case of Kevin and Mitch McGuire, Kevin was ashamed of his jealous feelings, but he also felt angry at his parents about the amount of time they spent caring for Mitch. A sibling who must spend most of his after school hours caring for a sibling with autism, who feels he cannot bring his friends home because of his sister's tantrums, and who is always the loser in competition for parental attention may feel a great deal of anger. Chapter 4 will discuss how balancing the needs of family members is a difficult but essential art.

It is important not to focus only on potential problems. There can be plenty of joy in a household that includes a child with a developmental disability. The other children can take pride in the achievements of the child with autism, for example, sharing in the sense of achievement when he learns to speak, participates in the Special Olympics, rides a bike with other kids, or learns to play cooperatively. The siblings should, of course, also have many opportunities to celebrate their own achievements. Growing up with a sibling with special needs can have positive as well as negative effects on your child. A family that copes effectively can rejoice in the achievements of every member, feel closer to one another because they know that have dealt well with difficult circumstances, and know the special pleasure that comes from realizing one can handle life's many challenges.

Adults will often say that their experiences as a sibling of a child with a handicapping condition, whether autism, mental retardation, or a mobility disorder, taught them a patience and tolerance they might not otherwise have learned. Being part of a family where there is a child with special needs can even influence one's vocational choices (Seligman & Darling, 1989). A brother may learn a sense of compassion from living with his sister with autism and carry this value into his adult life. For example, he may decide that he wishes to become a physician or a special education teacher. Several of my colleagues entered the field of autism because of first-hand experiences in their own families. I also know several siblings of children with autism who decided to become special education teachers or psychologists because of what they learned as children. By contrast, some children may feel they have given generously to their brother or sister and select an occupation that places few if any demands for human service. Either choice can be healthy if it is freely made.

Adulthood

I noted earlier that sibling relationships typically endure across the life span. Under the best of conditions this can mean the potential for intimate sharing with a beloved companion through one's life. However, when a sibling has autism it also means enduring responsibilities for that brother or sister. As long as parents are alive, the sibling role in care generally remains modest, and most mothers express a wish to buffer the sibling from significant responsibility (Holmes & Carr, 1991). However, after the death or incapacitation of a parent, this pattern must shift. In some families that may mean taking a sibling with autism into one's own adult home. For many families it means staying in touch with a sibling who resides in a group home or supervised apartment, and being available to handle the various problems that arise. These responsibilities may not be excessive or burdensome, and are often viewed as an act of love from one sibling to another. However, when combined with the needs of one's own children, one's aging parents, one's marriage, and work responsibilities, the continuing requirements of a brother or sister with autism can pose a significant additional demand. In addition, adults who have siblings with autism have shared with me their sense of sadness when, confronted by such painful events as the death of a parent, they could not seek solace from their brother or sister. Rather, they must bear the burden of their sorrow alone and respond to the on-going needs of their sibling as well.

For some siblings who failed to come to terms with their brother or sister with autism in childhood, adulthood offers new opportunities as well as new demands. Some people may enter adulthood without having understood the full range of the feelings they have toward a sibling with autism, or without having come to terms with these emotions. The feelings of anger, jealousy, or sadness they failed to deal with fully in childhood may linger and influence the adult's behavior. For example, one woman I know entered therapy because she could not get over the anger she felt toward her brother with autism whenever he came to her home. She realized the anger had less to do with her brother's current behavior than with the expectations she had carried from her childhood. An otherwise warm and compassionate woman, she was perplexed by her lack of patience with her brother and wished to free herself from her anger. A brief course of individual therapy enabled her to diminish her anger and to establish a new understanding of herself, her parents, and her brother.

For the adolescent or young adult looking forward to his or her own life, the anticipation of these responsibilities of caring for a sibling can cause considerable concern. A young adult may feel that she is expected to take in her brother to her own home, and wonder if anyone would want to marry her under those conditions. She may wonder if her own children will have autism and whether she should adopt instead of bearing children of her own. She may feel constrained from moving to another city because she feels responsible for her brother with autism. The more parents can help the young adult explore these feelings and concerns, the better it is likely to be for all involved. For example, a young woman who is apprehensive because she believes her parents expect her to bring her younger brother to live with her when they are no longer able to care for him, may be very much relieved to discover that her parents intend to help the young man make the transition to a group home, and simply hope his sister will look in on him from time to time. Chapter 3 focuses on communication skills that may help you explore these kinds of questions with your child.

Closing Comments

I have briefly examined the relationships between brothers and sisters, noting that some anger, competition, and resentment are normal in all relationships. Although the nature of sibling interaction changes over time, many people are fortunate enough to have an emotionally meaningful relationship with a sibling which will endure over time. For the brother or sister of a child with autism, creating a positive sibling bond may be more difficult than for other children. The child with autism has less capacity to be nurturing, or even to play with the normally developing child, may require a great deal more caretaking than other children, and does not follow the usual developmental path to increased independence. Although most children learn to cope effectively with their sibling's special needs, there is a great deal parents can do to help them with the process of adjustment. I will discuss those opportunities in the remainder of the book.

PARENTS SPEAK

Having an autistic sibling for Sam and Martha is very different. To some degree I think the birth order and personality of the sibling have an impact on what the relationship will be like. For example, Sam, being the older brother, has always seen Tommy as the baby. He has been understanding of Tom's needs, including all the extra time we have needed to spend with him. When Sam was younger he would get angry at Tom for touching his toys or messing up his room. As he matured he has shown compassion beyond his years. At times I think it has made him a kinder, gentler person.

Martha has had a more difficult time adjusting to Tommy. She is four years younger and he seemed to strike out more often at her. She experienced many problems dealing with him and it took a long time to get to the point we are at now. She has a great love for him but at the same time a fear of him. Even though she knows he is older, she thinks of him as her younger sibling.

Tommy has had a profound effect on his siblings and, like it or not, will probably to some extent shape who they are as adults.

When I was a kid it seemed to me my brother Rich, who has autism, got the lion's share of attention in our house. Now that I am an adult I can understand the jam my parents were in, but it was tough for me when I was younger. I love Rich, and my wife and I invite him to spend holidays with us, but I try to make sure my own kids understand why Uncle Rich needs so much of Dad's time when he visits.

I guess it isn't an accident that I ended up as a pediatrician. All the time I was growing up I kept praying there would be a way to cure Rich.

Stan is seven and has autism. His older sister, Sally, is nine. I worry a lot about what it means to grow up with a little brother like Stan. I want her to be able to bring her friends home and I don't want her to be afraid of him. I know our home has to be a little different than other homes, and I don't know how that will affect her emotionally as she grows up.

I think the thing that worries me most about Art is how he is going to feel about Jack as they grow up together. Here is Art, a little guy at age 5, telling his big brother Jack, who is 11, how to do things. I mean, what is he going to think about that as he gets older? Big brothers are supposed to take care of little guys, not the other way around. I'm concerned that it must be confusing to Art.

Justin is such a terrific kid. Sometimes I think he is almost too good. He spends so much time with his sister, Allie, who has autism. He acts like it is his job to do everything for her. I don't want him to resent that someday. To feel like she stole his childhood. I appreciate his help, but I don't want him to overdo. I'm not sure how much help is too much.

The Jansen Family

Tom Jansen looked at his youngest son's tear-stained face, and jumped from his chair, kneeling in front of the boy to fold him in his arms. Dick was crying, his clothes were dusty, and his hand was scraped. "What is it son? What happened?" At first Dick was sobbing too hard to answer, but gradually in the comfort of his father's arms he began to calm down and tell his story.

Earlier that Saturday morning Dick's mom had sent him to the barbershop two short blocks away, and on his way he met some kids from school. He recognized them, but they were in the sixth grade, and he was in the third grade, so he did not think they knew him. Then, one of the boys called out to him, "Hey Dick, what you doing?" Dick smiled shyly, flattered to be noticed by the older boy, and said he was going to get his hair cut. Catching his arm, the boy told Dick to stop a minute, and then he began to ask him about his brother. "What's the matter with that dumb old brother of yours anyhow? How come he always acts so weird?" Dick became indignant. "Leave my brother out of this. He's OK and he never bothers you." The older boys laughed. "If you think he's OK, then you're pretty weird too!" Dick turned around and tried to push one of his tormentors away. The boys laughed again, pushed Dick in the dust, and walked away.

Dick began to choke with tears as the words flooded out to his father, "What's wrong with Mal? Why won't he talk? Maybe he just doesn't want to. The guys are right, Daddy. He acts so weird sometimes. I just want him to be a regular brother. I know you said Mal has autism, but why does he have to be so weird? I stood up for him, but I don't understand why he is that way." The words tumbled out until, out of breath and angry-sad, Dick finally stopped.

Tears came to Tom Jansen's eyes as he listened to the story. Poor little guy. What a tough time he was having. When Tom and his wife, Alice, moved to this neighborhood they worried about how it would be for Dick to grow up as one of a handful of African-American youngsters in a mostly white community. Thankfully, with the exception of a couple of unpleasant incidents, that had not been a major issue. But, now instead of racism, there were all the burdens of growing up with a brother with autism. With a sense of deep sadness, Tom realized that just as he was helping Dick learn how to deal with the racism he sometimes met in his daily life, so too did he need to help him understand autism and learn how to handle other people's reactions. It might not be fair for Dick to have to carry these burdens, but they were his nonetheless, and he would have to learn how to handle them.

Introduction

Dick Jansen's encounter with intolerance for persons with autism is not unique to him. Many of us have had similar experiences, where other people have revealed their offensive misunderstanding of autism. It might be a neighbor who yells at your child for venturing into his yard, or a stranger in a supermarket who criticizes you when your child has a tantrum, or an uncle who suggests you should either leave your child home, or not come to his family picnics. These experiences may leave you angry, sad, and frightened. However upsetting other people's behavior may be, at least you understand the truth about your child, and so you are less vulnerable to these verbal assaults than is a child. Other children, just like adults, will sometimes respond to a person with a disability out of fear, ignorance, or meanness. That kind of experience can be painful for anyone in a family, but especially for children. It is one of life's brutal moments.

In his distress about his experience, Dick also revealed that he understood very little about what was wrong with his brother. For example, he wondered if Mal just did not want to talk. That kind of statement indicates how little Dick understood about autism. Tom would have to help Dick understand what autism is, feel confident of his factual information, and handle the insults, intentional or accidental, that he might encounter on behalf of his brother. Discrimination on any grounds is wrong, and it is always destructive, but it may be a little easier to bear and to fight against when a person feels self-confident and knowledgeable. Dick had no words to fight back against his tormentors, because he himself did not understand Mal. So, although he loyally tried to defend his brother, he was overwhelmed by his confusion.

Although many children will respond to another child's physical or mental disability with curiosity, kindness, or matter-of-fact acceptance, others may react with ignorance, fear, or even with cruelty. For the sibling of a child with autism, these negative reactions can be one more painful demand in the process of growing up with a brother or sister who has special needs. As a parent you cannot anticipate all of the problems that might arise in the world of childhood, nor can you protect your children from all of the unhappiness they will confront, but with some planning on your part it is possible to help siblings understand autism and know how to cope with another child's curious or hurtful response.

Combating ignorance and educating others is an important skill for a sibling. However, it is even more important that she understand autism for her own emotional well-being. The sibling of a child with autism must know about the disorder. Ignorance about autism can breed fear, and fear can damage a child's sense of herself and her relationship with her brother or sister. For example, a sister might tease her brother with autism, as she would any other child, and then feel conscience-stricken over mistreating him. Similarly, she might feel guilty about jealous or angry reactions to her brother. She needs to know what autism is, and she needs to understand her responses to her brother's condition, so she will be at ease with herself and with him.

To help your children be well informed about autism, accepting of themselves and their sibling, and able to fend for themselves in the world of childhood you must be able to discuss the disorder in a way that is meaningful to the child. Precisely how you do that will vary with your child's stage of development. This chapter addresses how to explain autism to children of different ages. As you will soon see, a child's age is an important factor in what kinds of information you should share.

In your eagerness to inform your child, do not make the mistake of imposing too much at one time. For example, if your daughter asks why her brother repeats back what other people say to him rather than answering their questions, she will be content with a brief answer about his echolalia (parroting of speech) and is not asking for an extended discussion of autism. You might say something like, "He repeats what I said because he does not know the answer to my question. When he gets older he will repeat less because he will know more words to answer with."

Offer information as questions arise, mention the topic of autism from time to time, but do not overdo the educating. Children usually want some specific information to address a problem that has arisen. Often they will signal that they are satisfied with your answer by changing the topic, asking if they are done, or telling you outright that they do not wish to hear anymore just now. Respect that. You have an entire childhood in which to help your child learn what he needs to know.

The Impact of Development on Children's Understanding of Autism

Parents have sometimes said to me that they told their child about autism at a very early age and that their child understood. Indeed, at three or four years of age, a younger sibling might say, "My brother has autism." This seeming understanding may create a false sense of security for parents who believe that they have established a family atmosphere in which there are no secrets, and the children are fully informed about autism. It may then be puzzling when they discover that their children seem misinformed and confused about the disorder. One mother told me that although the word "autism" had been used around her home since her daughter was born, she was surprised one day when the girl, then six years old, came to her and said, "Mommy, what is autism, really?" We saw this same perplexity in the case of Dick Jansen, who knew his brother had autism, but had little idea what the term meant.

Psychologists who study child development would not be surprised that a child could grow up with the word "autism" as a household term and still not understand what it is about. Children are able to use words well before they understand them, and a boy of three or four years who says that his sister has autism may mean no more by that than that she stares at lights or does not talk. The concept of autism is quite abstract and will not be fully understood by a child until a much older age. As a result, it is important to present the information you share with children in ways that are developmentally appropriate, and to repeat the information many times over the years, in increasingly mature and complex language as the child grows up. These lessons about autism are to be taught many times.

For the Young Child

Most parents understand the importance of adjusting information to a child's age when they offer sex education. The simple ideas we share with young children about "where babies come from" are quite different from the more complex information we would offer an adolescent. Similarly, for the very young child, autism will only be understood in relation to specific, concrete behaviors. The two-year-old is focused on questions of "what" and may endlessly ask for names of objects. For a child this age, autism is lining up all the toy cars in a row, or throwing cereal on the floor, or riding in a yellow school bus. Although you might use the word "autism" in a conversation with a child this young, he has no ability to understand the word. His world is focused on specific behaviors and he will respond to those behaviors, positive and negative, as they occur.

It is not uncommon for children with autism to have a tantrum, demonstrate stereotyped, repetitive (self-stimulatory) behaviors such as finger waving or light gazing, or be aggressive toward other people. These behaviors can be a source of distress for the entire family and may be a special cause of concern for siblings. A little girl may be terrified of her brother's tantrums or aggression, both frightened for her own safety and perplexed by his behavior. Very young children in particular may be alarmed by what they rightly perceive to be out of control behavior on the part of another child.

Explanations will be of relatively little use, but concrete intervention may help. For example, if she is frightened by her brother's tantrums, she must be comforted and reassured. Later, if she can be encouraged to play simple games like rolling a ball to her brother, and she enjoys the game, that will be good for both children. The fact that her brother has autism has no meaning to a two- or three-year-old.

The typical four–year-old is filled with questions, ranging from why the sky is blue to why she has to go to bed. Parents know that these questions can sometimes go on in an endless chain. Child: "Why is the grass green?" Adult: "Because it looks so pretty." (Or, God made it green. Or, it has special green color in it.) Child: "Why does it look so pretty?" And so forth, sometimes for as long as our patience holds out! Her curiosity seems endless. If she has a brother with autism she may ask why he cannot talk. She will probably accept that his silence occurs because her brother has autism, but certainly will have no capacity to understand on a more abstract level what the concept of autism means. Indeed, she is likely to be quite content with the simplest possible explanation. Although the word "autism" might be used by a child of this age, she should not be expected to understand the term any more than if she were told that chlorophyll makes the grass green. So, answers to questions must be kept simple. For example, you might say that her brother is crying because he is afraid, or he does not talk because he has not learned how, or he waves his hands because he is excited. These simple explanations are specific, factual, and concrete.

By the age of six or seven years, the young child will use "because" in his language and offer simple explanations of physical events. However, his explanations may be based on mistaken assumptions. For example, he may have two friends who are the same age, but assume one is older because she is taller. Children of this age engage in a great deal of fantasy and magical thinking. This ability to pretend is both part of the wonder and part of the torment of childhood. For example, a child may begin to concoct stories about a sibling's autism. A boy might tell himself that his brother's autism came from getting sick, because once the boy heard someone refer to his brother's condition as a sickness. The next step in his childish logic might lead him to fear that if he gets sick, he too could "get autism." Similarly, a little girl who has been jealous and angry toward her baby brother may wish he would go live in another family. She might be guilt stricken when he is diagnosed with autism because her "bad thoughts" gave him autism. Parents need to reassure children about these fears, just as we show them there are no monsters lurking in the closet or hiding under the bed. We need to correct their mistaken logic, giving them the simple facts they need, such as that they cannot catch autism as they might a cold.

For very young children, parents can expect to deal with feelings of fear, anger, or jealousy. Children at this age need to be comforted when afraid, helped to regain their control when angry, and given enough attention to minimize jealous feelings. For example, a child who is frightened by the odd behaviors of his older sibling should be reassured that he is safe, and physically removed from the area if the child with autism is engaging in tantrums or aggressive behavior which might be harmful. A sibling who is angry because the child with autism has done something to upset him such as taking his toys or knocking over his blocks needs to be helped to find words to express his anger, and then provided with appropriate restitution. For example, if the blocks were knocked over, his father might offer to rebuild them, or the child might be directed toward another attractive play activity. Similarly, the sibling who is jealous of the child with autism needs help in expressing these feelings and reassurance about how valued he himself is to the parents. Remember too that feelings such as fear, anger, and jealousy are normal feelings of early childhood and would be present to some extent even if there were not a child with autism in the family.

If the tantrums of the child with autism are frightening or endangering a young sibling, provisions must be made for that child's safety. For example, when a child begins to tantrum in the presence of the sibling, it is helpful if you can take immediate steps to separate the children. You might calmly ask the normally developing sibling to leave the room, saying "Tom is having trouble controlling himself right now. I need to work with him. It will help me a lot if you will go into the living room and watch your video until he is calm." After the tantrum has ended, you should seek out the sibling, discuss what happened, and explore how he felt.

Parents should plan with a sibling what to do if a brother or sister with autism becomes aggressive or destructive while they are alone together. The child should be told that helping her brother learn to control his tantrums is a job for a grown up, not a child. This draws a clear boundary between the re-sponsibilities of children and adults. For example, a child may be told to walk away and call Mom or Dad for help. After the fa-ther has handled the immediate crisis of the tantrum, he should touch base with the sibling. Thus, he might say, "I'm glad you came to get me when Rich started to throw your cars. I know how scary that can be. Maybe it made you mad too. I'm sorry it happened to you. Your mom and I will teach Rich how to play with cars instead of throwing them. But, un-til he learns that, we will keep you safe."

Young children enjoy using dolls, hand puppets, or other toys to learn about autism or deal with their emotions about their brother or sister. Fantasy play is a primary means of ex-pressing feelings in the early years, and parents can encour-age children to voice a problem and reach solutions through play and story telling. For example, a child who is upset by the tantrums of his sister may find it helpful to use hand puppets to play act the events and see how they are resolved by the puppet who plays the parent role. Similarly, making up a story that has a solution to a troubling problem may help the child resolve a difficulty. Sometimes a child will play act the same events many times until he has mastered the solution.

For the child of six or seven years, creating a book with pictures cut out from a magazine and a text dictated by the child may be a helpful way to summarize for them what they know about their brother's or sister's autism. For example, seven-year-old Joe wrote a book with his parents entitled "Joe and Jack." It was about Joe and his brother Jack, who had autism. Joe cut out pictures from a magazine of children playing, and he asked his mother to write down the following words, "Joe and Jack are brothers. Joe likes to play, but Jack doesn't know how to play. Jack has autism. That makes Joe sad because he wants to play ball with Jack. Mommy says maybe Jack can learn to play with Joe. Dad will teach Jack how to play ball with Joe. This is a true story. The End."

Middle Childhood

Children of middle childhood, from about 9 to 12 years of age, collect vast amounts of information and may be a storehouse of facts about autism. They can typically understand that it is a problem of the brain, that it is not "catching," that their sibling needs special education services, and so forth. If their sibling has mental retardation they will understand that this is an enduring problem. They can shed many of the misconceptions they may have had as younger children and become increasingly mature in their discussion of the disorder. Parents will want to watch for receptive moments to offer information. Although some children will ask questions, parents may also initiate the discussion. Examples of potentially fruitful times for talking would include times when the child with autism is making a transition such as starting a new school, a report of progress from the child's teacher, or a disruptive episode that has upset the sibling.

Children of middle childhood are starting the process of separating from their family, and focusing more of their social and emotional world in their peer group. Although adolescence is still in the offing, the building blocks for greater independence are being put in place. Children of this age will be joining clubs, going to slumber parties, and finding best friends. This increased independence means they will spend less time at home, and they may have less interest in playing with a younger sibling, or one who has autism. At the same time that they are maturing socially and emotionally, they are also changing intellectually and are capable of a more complex understanding of autism.

This maturing understanding of autism has the potential to collide with their dawning interest in a wider social experience, because as they start to understand the disability and its impact, they may feel more obligated to take care of their sibling. As a result it is important that a child's concern for her sibling not keep her too closely tied to home. Children of this age need to be encouraged to pursue their many interests beyond the home and family. This exploration of the world's possibilities and discovery of their own skills and abilities makes this a potentially delightful stage of childhood.

Their growing reliance on their peer group can also make children of middle childhood very vulnerable to the reactions of other children concerning their sibling with autism. Some children of this age may begin to turn away from their sibling with autism in an effort to fit in with their peers. That behavior may be disconcerting to parents, especially when it comes from a child who has been very loving up until that time. Understanding that the changes in attitude reflect a developmental process may enable parents to be more patient, while still helping their daughter understand that her rejection of her brother is not acceptable.

One father called me in distress when he discovered that his daughter was calling her brother with autism a "dummy," and laughing with her friends. His first impulse was to yell at her, and take away privileges. But, as we talked about his daughter's efforts to become part of her peer group, he changed his approach. Understanding that his daughter's embarrassment and subsequent rejection of her brother were normal for her age made it easier for him to decide on an effective response. Although conveying clearly his disapproval of her behavior, he also encouraged her to think about what she was doing and why she was doing it. With his patient guidance, her "bad behavior" was turned into a lesson in growing up. He also discussed with her how she could respond to her friends. For example, he suggested that if they called her brother a "dummy" she might say, "You think he's a dummy because you don't know him. Tom has autism and so he can't talk well. He goes to a school where he's learning a lot of things. He is really good with puzzles and things." Her father also suggested that if they asked questions she did not know how to answer, she could tell them she would check with her parents and let them know. He was also very much aware of how easily young people are embarrassed in front of their friends and took pains only to correct her when they were alone.

Children of middle childhood also become increasingly aware of their parents as "flawed" persons who can make mistakes. As a result they may begin to be critical of their parents for many things including how they are dealing with the child with autism. This is the time in childhood when parents begin to lose their heroic stature and start to be recognized as the mortal beings they actually are. There is no harm in acknowledging to children that you do not have all the answers. In the case of autism, as in so many of life's questions, no one knows all the answers. It is not essential that children see parents as all knowing. To the contrary, they need a realistic sense of their parents as people who are able to cope with a problem in spite of the difficulties they face. This provides the growing child with a realistic model, rather than a superhero whose achievements can never be equalled by the youngster growing up.

As parents begin to diminish in their absolute authority and wisdom, so too will their power to provide comfort and reassurance to the child diminish. As discussed in Chapter 1, while children will still seek their parents for consolation, more of their emotional needs will start to be met by their friends. This transition to adolescence may help prepare parents and children for the more active process of separation that occurs in the teenage years.

Adolescence

It is not until adolescence that young people become intellectually capable of understanding autism as fully as does an adult. The adolescent should have access to as much information about autism as he wishes, although it is important for parents to remember that factual understanding and emotional acceptance are different processes. We have all had the experience of yearning for things that we know are not possible. For example, a young person may understand intellectually that his brother's autism is an enduring problem, but still be reluctant to accept that limit on an emotional basis. He will need his parents' support in accepting the full impact of his sibling's disability (see Chapter 3). Thus, the difficult challenge for parents at this age is not explaining autism. The young person has a mature ability to grasp fact and theory. What is challenging is helping the teenager understand what autism means for himself, his family, and his brother or sister.

The adolescent who likes to read may find a book about autism in the family library and read it on his own. Perhaps he will write an essay for an English class about his sister with autism, and he may include some of his own feelings in his written work. It will differ from a paper he might have written a few years earlier, because it will be more than a listing of facts. Rather, it may include an appreciation of theories about the cause of autism, or a thoughtful reflection on the emotional impact of autism on his life and that of the family. He will be able to separate out the effects of autism and mental retardation, and see how each of these affects his brother's development.

With older children, especially adolescents, questions arise about their role in managing the disruptive behavior. My own view is that older siblings can play a role in a program which involves positive reinforcement for appropriate behavior or a very mild punishment such as saying "No" or withdrawing one's attention as a consequence for inappropriate behavior. However, most siblings will not be emotionally or physically able to use procedures such as physical restraint should that be necessary. In addition, it is essential that punishments not be used by people who do not know how to apply them correctly or who might misuse them. These techniques are difficult for adults to do, and may be too much for a child to handle. It is much better to err on the side of caution than to place too much responsibility on a child.

Except under very unusual conditions, parents, not siblings, are responsible for disciplining children. This is true in every family, not only those who include a child with autism. However, when an adolescent child is left in charge for brief periods, for example during an evening when parents have gone to dinner, the older child needs to have the authority to manage the younger. If such authority places too much of a demand on the older child, a paid respite worker, member of the extended family, or sitter should be hired for the younger child. A teacher or psychologist can play a useful role in helping parents think about these issues in relation to their children.

The adolescent has the capacity to reflect on past and future, and may begin to grapple with questions of her adult responsibility for the sibling with autism. Similarly, the question of whether she might herself give birth to a child with autism may become an important issue for the teenager. Because these questions of adult responsibility and child bearing are so common among adolescents, parents will want to raise the topics and share information if their teenager is receptive. Questions about the transmission of autism may sometimes need to be answered by a genetic counselor who is familiar with autism and knows the current research on its inheritance.

These personal concerns may be very difficult for a young person to express because she does not want to upset her parents or perhaps because she is ashamed of, or embarrassed by, the thoughts. She may well reveal more of her thoughts to her best friend than to her parents. This is a natural part of growing up. That increased privacy does not mean she has become inaccessible to her parents, but it does signal that they will have to be alert to her needs and recognize the times when communication is possible. Many parents tell me that relaxed, private time is the best opportunity they have to initiate this kind of conversation with a child. For example, a drive in the car, or a Sunday morning around the breakfast table, may be opportunities to begin a discussion.

Teenagers have the capacity to understand the distress experienced by their parents and be attuned to emotional issues that might escape the younger child. For example, a teenage son may see the flicker of pain in his father's eye when a younger sister with autism turns away from his greeting as he comes home from work. This can teach him something about his father's life. However, it could also make the continuing process of adolescent separation from the family more difficult, because the teenager may feel that he needs to remain close to home to meet his parents' emotional needs. For example, a young woman might announce that she wishes to attend a local community college rather than living two hours away at the state university. Similarly, after having dreamed from childhood of joining the Air Force, a young man might suddenly say that he is going to stay home and work in a local factory. There are many reasons why young people might change their plans or stick too close to home, but if there is a sibling with autism, parents should be alert to that as a possible factor in decision making. Open discussion of the issue, and encouragement to develop her own life, may allow the young person to pursue her dreams. Setting the stage for this discussion is described in Chapter 3.

If your teenager is unable to make his way toward an independent life because he feels too responsible for you and his brother, you may want to consult with a psychologist or other therapist for help in teaching the entire family how to shift its patterns of interaction. Similarly, the teenager who appears disconnected from his sister with autism and who reflects his pain through rebellion or chronic anger may benefit from such help.

Adulthood

The adult sibling of a person with autism may assume a variety of roles in relation to her parents and her sibling. As a mature woman she will have the opportunity to understand the emotional experiences of her parents, and to support them in their plans for her brother with autism. This support can ease the concerns of aging parents about the future of their son and may be a link that strengthens their emotional connection with their daughter. She may gradually assume increased responsibility for overseeing his welfare. Taking on greater responsibility requires that she be fully informed about such things as behavior management, community resources, and medical needs of her sibling. It is important that she have the full benefit of her parents' experience so that she does not have to start at ground zero when she becomes responsible for him. Over the years, as her parents age, and ultimately die, she may become her brother's legal guardian. For the higher functioning person with autism, this oversight may be more modest; nonetheless, even those people with autism who function quite independently may still benefit from a supportive hand from time to time.

The death of a parent is an inevitable part of normal family life and a time of pain and sorrow as children cope with an unavoidable life tragedy. I had a conversation at a conference with Ronald A., a middle-aged man who has an older sister with autism. He shared with me how his grief at the loss of his parents was intensified by the needs of his sister. Mr. A.'s parents both died within 18 months of each other, creating a great deal of emotional and physical stress. Mr. A. had his own family to care for, including two children who were grieving the loss of beloved grandparents. He also had to respond to the medical crisis which preceded each parent's death, make the funeral arrangements, and settle his parents' estate. Each of these is a wrenching, difficult experience. What intensified the process for Mr. A. was that he also abruptly became responsible for overseeing the care of his sister. She lived in a group home in the town where her parents resided and he had to decide whether she should remain there or move closer to him so he could provide closer supervision of her welfare. It hit him with full force that he was fully responsible for her and always would be. Thus, the normal anguish that accompanies the death of a parent was compounded for Mr. A. by the special needs of his sister.

Part of life's richness is our ever-growing capacity to comprehend the significance of what happens to us. This does not mean the experiences are always positive. There can be a justified sense of burden and real sorrow attached to being the sibling of a person with autism. The elder brother of a man with autism confided in me that it was not until his father died, and he felt the full weight of responsibility for overseeing his brother's welfare, that he really understood what his parents had given all of their children in love and support. He also realized how much they had sacrificed to achieve those goals.

You may not be physically present in your child's life when she achieves that level of understanding about autism, and about her relationship with her brother and with you, but the gifts of love, support, and wisdom you shared with her across the years of her childhood will endure and form the matrix of her mature understanding.

Closing Comments

In sum, there is a vast difference between the 5–year-old who announces that "My brother has autism" and the 15–year-old who does the same. What the young child and the adolescent mean conceptually and what they experience emotionally about the idea of autism will be markedly different. Part of effective parenting is recognizing these differences and making your explanations fit the developmental needs of the child. You may not always have the answers to your child's questions. When you do not, a good book such as *Children with Autism* (Powers, 1989) or a call to the local autism society chapter may give you the information you need. Being prepared with age-appropriate information leads parents to the next challenge, that of communicating effectively with their child. You need to know both what to say and how to say it. Chapter 3 discusses some fundamentals of parent-child communication skills.

PARENTS SPEAK

Over the years my children and I have many times discussed Tom's disabilities—not so much in clinical terms but in terms of their feelings about him.

There are times we need to explain Tommy's behavior to neighbors or friends and that can be difficult, especially for the children. Martha explains everything away by saying, "Tom is just handicapped." Sam will go into more detail to try to get the other person to understand Tommy's difficulties. Rather than define autism, he describes Tommy as the child he is.

Today, when I stand back and take a hard look at Annie's understanding of Matt's autism, I realize it has been a gradual process for her. As early as age three, Annie questioned why Matt wouldn't answer her or play with her. I would explain to her that Matt was still "learning to talk" or still "learning to play." Then I would prompt from Matt some speech or play directed toward Annie.

As Annie grew closer to five years old, her questions regarding Matt increased and grew more complex ("Why does Matt need help talking?" and "Why can't he go to my school?"). I told her that Matt had difficulty learning to speak and doing certain things because of something called "autism." I explained to her that Matt was born with autism, as were other children in his school.

Annie wanted to know if he would "always be like this." I answered her by saying I didn't know exactly what Matt would be like when he was older. I did know that we would continue to work very hard with him. I told her that together we had already helped Matt so much. I let her know how very proud I was of her. I knew sometimes it was difficult for her. Matt put a lot of demands on my time, and there were times when she was in uncomfortable situations because of his behaviors. I gave her time to speak about those feelings.

Lastly, I reminded her that we were a family, and that meant she was not alone. I told her that we were fortunate to be able to talk to each other about everything, whenever we needed to. Then I said, "I love you so very much," and she repeated those words back to me, and gave me her biggest hug.

The hardest thing for me to understand is how to give a simple answer to my daughter's questions about her brother's autism. I talk too much and sometimes turn it into a lecture. But when I go into too much detail she will just wander away and go back to her play. She is teaching me when to stop!

Ellen is 15 and goes to the regional high school. This year they had a class assignment in English to write about their personal hero. I was moved to tears when I read her essay. She had written about her younger brother Seth who is nine and has autism. She wrote about how hard he has struggled to learn to talk and how brave he seems to her, always trying to get beyond his autism.

Zack is only five and Jeff, who is autistic, is seven. Zack asks things like why Jeff won't play with him or why he won't talk. I give him simple answers like "he still has to learn how to talk." I hope that is enough.

We have gone through some hard times since my daughter entered junior high school. She seems to be embarrassed by me, her father, and her brother Jack. She doesn't want to be seen with Jack, whose behavior can be quite disruptive. My husband and I are thinking of some counseling for her.

I remember when I was a senior in high school and we had to do our senior term paper. I decided to write mine on what causes autism. Although I had grown up with a sister who has autism and watched my parents cope with her every day, I never really understood what made her that way. So I wrote this paper on what made people autistic. I couldn't believe some of the stuff I read about how parents made their kids that way and I got really upset. I knew my parents were too great for that. Then I found this book in the library by a guy named Bernard Rimland. It was all about how autism was probably caused by damage to the brain. That made a lot of sense to me. Remember, this was a lot of years ago, back in the late '60s, before all the great research that has been done.

3

LET'S TALK: Helping Children Share Their Thoughts and Feelings

The Martin Family

Rosemary Martin glanced around the kitchen table. Her 11–year-old daughter, Kathy, smiled back, 13–year-old Rich looked up from the book he was reading, and 20–year-old Joe sat quietly at the end of the table, carefully inspecting his hands. Rosemary nodded at her husband, Dan, and he smiled as he said, "OK, time to call this meeting of the Martin family to order. Looks like everyone is present and accounted for."

Rich put down his book, saying, "Yo, dad, what's up?" Dan grinned at his younger boy, and began to explain why he and Rosemary had called this family meeting. They wanted to talk about plans for Joe, who would be graduating from school in June. When he was 5 years old Joe had been diagnosed as having autism, and he had spent the past 15 years in special education programs. Thanks to a lot of patient teaching at home and in school, Joe had made impressive progress. But, in spite of all he was able to learn, it was also clear that he would continue to need some special services throughout his life. His speech was still limited, he sometimes got very uncomfortable in unfamiliar situations, and he had a lot of difficulty interacting with other people. But, he was a neat, careful worker who knew how to use handtools and office *equipment. He had excellent self-care skills and was a big help at home. Joe also was good natured and easy to live with unless something really major happened to upset his routines. It was very important to Joe that he keep things in order.*

Rosemary said she wanted the children to understand the plans they had for Joe, where he would live and where he would work. Graduation from school would mean changes in Joe's life and for everyone else, so everyone in the family should be aware of what was being planned and have an opportunity to share in the discussion. Rosemary and Dan had talked with Joe many times to help him understand that his school days would soon be at an end, and his teacher at school was doing the same. Their parents had also shared some of this with Kathy and Rich as well and told each of them that Joe would be moving to a group home, but they had not talked as a whole family about the future, and it was important for them to do so.

When Dan said that they had put Joe's name on a waiting list for a group home in their community, Kathy got upset. She said she wanted Joe to live with her all her life, and she could not understand how her parents could think about sending him away. Dan gently reminded her that when most young people grow up, they leave their parents' home and find a place of their own. The fact that Joe had autism did not mean he could not be independent, just as Kathy and Rich would be when they got older. Dan said that he knew how much Kathy loved her brother, and that he hoped she would always spend time with him and make sure things were going OK for him. But he went on to say that when she grew up Kathy would have her own husband and children to share her home. Joe would probably be happier in his own place as well, with friends to share activities, and a group home supervisor to advise him when he needed extra help or support.

Joe had been very quiet during most of this conversation, looking at his hands, and occasionally rocking gently for a few seconds. A couple of times he echoed "Go to the group home" after his mother or father used the words, but he had not made any other comments. After Kathy had stopped crying and dried her eyes, he looked over at her and said "Kathy's smiling."

When Kathy had recovered from her distress and the family was feeling more relaxed, Rosemary said that one of the things she and Dan wanted to do to celebrate Joe's graduation from school, and increasing independence, was to plan a family event. They wondered what the children would like to do to celebrate Joe's graduation. Rich laughed and said, "How about a trip around the world?" Kathy, who had volunteered to be secretary for their brainstorming session, wrote that down, and then volunteered an idea of her own, "I'd like to take a trip to Washington. Maybe we would see the president." Rich chimed in again, "Let's think about going skiing. We could go out west." Dan suggested a trip to one of the islands to go scuba diving, and Rosemary responded that would be great as long as they had horseback riding too. When Dan asked Joe what he would like to do, Joe replied "Go camp" and Kathy said, "Yeah Dad, let's go camping in the mountains like we did last summer."

After a few more minutes of generating ideas, Dan suggested they had a good list of possibilities, and now they could go back and see which one would work best. After more discussion they all agreed that since it was Joe's graduation he should have the biggest voice in what they did, and so they decided to go camping. Finally, Dan commented that it been a long meeting and it was nearly time to wrap it up. "Just to remind you, first we talked about where Joe will be living and working next year. He is on a waiting list for a group home and should be able to move there within six to nine months. I'll give them a call and see if we can all stop by for a visit some time soon so you kids can have a look at it. He is also going to start in a job training program after he graduates from school. But, we also agreed that as soon as he graduates we are going to have a family celebration and spend a week camping."

As they were about to leave the table, Kathy got teary eyed again. "Mom, are you sure we will be able to see Joe after he moves to the new place?" Rosemary gave her a hug and assured her that Joe would always be her big brother. He would visit them on weekends and they would go to see him in his new home. There would be family vacations, holidays, and many times to visit.

Introduction

Good communication is vital to a happy family. Parents and children need to be able to tell one another what they are thinking and feeling. They also need to be able to sit down together to discuss problems and agree on solutions that meet the needs of the entire family. This does not mean that everyone will be completely satisfied with the outcome. A lot of compromise is sometimes needed in family problem solving, and sometimes parents must make decisions that are not popular with children. Not every child will respond to her parents' reassurance as well as Kathy Martin did when she became upset about Joe going into the group home. However, open, honest communication can increase the likelihood that everyone will feel his or her opinion was heard.

Part of effective parenting is creating an atmosphere where that kind of communication is possible. That means teaching children the skills that lead to the open exchange of ideas and creating situations where they can practice these skills. Children who learn from their parents how to communicate well with the people they love will find those skills hold them in good stead all of their lives. Not only will they be happier with the family of their childhood, they should also be able to carry these same skills into their adulthood and pass them on to their own children.

As we just saw in the case of the Martin family, sometimes parents may call for a family meeting to give the entire family a chance to hear important information and share in decision making. Dan and Rosemary Martin were confronted by a major event in the life of their oldest boy, Joe. Joe was graduating from school in a few months and it was necessary for his parents to make plans for the next step in his life. Although they had thought about this event for many years, and had started to make plans in Joe's early adolescence, as the time grew close they had to take concrete action to make arrangements for their son. Ideally, the Martins might have done better if they had talked earlier as a family about the options for Joe and explored the idea of a group home more fully. But this was an emotionally laden process and Dan and Rosemary had to prepare themselves first.

There were many painful moments in planning for Joe's future. Knowing that he was about to turn 21 years old was a powerful symbol for Rosemary and Dan. They felt a renewed sense of sadness when they thought about what a 21st birthday meant for other young men who would be graduating from college, launching a career, and perhaps getting married. None of these pleasures would ever belong to Joe. However, they were also proud of Joe's achievements and wanted to celebrate his manhood with him. They knew how hard he had worked to gain his education and to learn to manage the effects of his autism. After they had shared their feelings, happy and sad, with one another, and made the decisions they knew had to made by them as Joe's parents, they felt ready to include their children in some of the decision making.

The Martins knew that their other children would feel some distress over the idea of Joe's move to a group home. However, as his parents they believed it was the best plan for Joe and for them. They were committed to the idea, but wanted the children to understand what they were doing. They also wanted the children to feel that Joe was entering adulthood, an event to celebrate, and therefore wanted the whole family to join in planning the celebration.

Later in the chapter I will discuss some of the procedures the Martins followed to make their family meeting an effective one. Before I do that, I am going to consider some of the obstacles that make communication between parents and children difficult, and how you can create an atmosphere that makes it easier to communicate. Family communication when there is a child with autism is made additionally complex because of such factors as time demands, difficulties of behavior management, and sibling issues that arise. Each family establishes its own style, its own customs, and rituals, but knowing some of the pitfalls and possibilities of how families communicate may give you ideas you can adapt to your own situation.

Creating an Atmosphere for Communication

Most of us value those relationships we have had over the years with other persons who seemed able to look into our hearts. These were people who listened closely to us, understood our words, encouraged us to discover who we were, and sometimes helped us understand ourselves a bit better. We flourish in those relationships, growing more open, sharing our feelings, and knowing ourselves better. Good parents do that; so do good friends and good psychotherapists. Love alone is not enough to accomplish that goal. Loving your child is important to good communication, but there are other things you can do as well to help the sharing process.

Good listening skills are essential to creating an atmosphere where your child will feel able to reveal personal thoughts and feelings to you. In the following pages I will consider both some of the barriers that might make it harder for parents and children to communicate about autism, and some of the specific skills you could use to help your child feel more at ease in sharing experiences and in communicating with his brother or sister. People who use these skills tell me they are helpful not only in talking to their children, but also to their spouse, their friends, and their co-workers.

Barriers to Communication

Although most parents would like to communicate effectively with their children about a sibling's autism, there may be barriers that make this sharing difficult. One barrier is the emotional reactions parents may feel about the impact of autism on the life of a cherished child. It is quite common for parents to feel such emotions as deep sadness, loss, or anger about their child's autism. These feelings are a normal response to the tragic effect of autism on a child's development.

Parents may fear revealing negative feelings to their children because they are ashamed of the feelings, think they are abnormal, or because they do not wish to burden the children with their emotions. Unfortunately, it is difficult to keep our feelings secret, especially from our family, who share our home and see our moods on a daily basis. Although a child may not understand the reason why Dad is sad or Mom is angry, she is very likely to pick up on the feelings. She will notice the sadness in your face, the edge of anger in your voice, your lack of pleasure in the small things, or your preoccupation with your own thoughts.

Most of us cannot conceal the clues to our real feelings. Your child will notice these changes in you and react to them. If she has no other explanation, she may attribute your distress to something she did, and she may begin to blame herself for some imagined offense. Every child does little things that make her feel guilty. These are often minor infractions that are unimportant to us as adults. However, in her mind these childish misbehaviors can loom large and be magnified into the reason for your distress. As we saw in Chapter 2, sometimes a child can frighten herself with the things she imagines.

Clearly, parents do not wish to burden children with the full intensity of their feelings of grief, anxiety, or disappointment about a sibling's autism. Such feelings are best shared between husband and wife as Dan and Rosemary Martin did, by friends, minister, priest or rabbi, or professional therapist. However, children can understand that parents feel a range of emotions. They can accept that sadness, anger, or regret may be among the many reactions, along with love, concern, and other positive feelings parents experience in relation to a child.

When parents label their own emotions, explain that they are linked to feelings of concern for the child with autism, but do not diminish their love for that child, or for the other children, this may help to ease siblings' concerns about an adult's emotional state. At the very least, your child will know she is not the cause of your distress, and she can realistically label your feelings as due to other events in your life. You can share "good" feelings as well as "bad," both when your child comments on your behavior and when she does not. Very young children need simple labels like "happy," "sad," or "mad," while older children can deal with more complex feelings of frustration, sorrow, or exhilaration. Although labeling of these feelings is important, parents are also entitled to the privacy of their own feelings, and you should respect your own needs just as you do those of your child. Share what you are able, but do not feel obligated to share what you need to keep private.

An example of appropriate sharing of adult feelings was described to me by a mother who has been preoccupied with finding a school for her young son with autism and who realized that she has not paid much attention to her older daughter. She made it a point to find a time for special sharing, by taking her daughter to lunch on Saturday afternoon while her husband spent time with their son. During their lunch she said, "I feel like I've really missed spending time with you the last few weeks. I've been so worried about finding the right school for Donnie, that I could not be with you as much as I like to. So, I really wanted to be sure we had some special time together today. How has it been going for you?" Her daughter basked in the warmth of special attention, and both of them enjoyed their time together.

In addition to wishing to protect children from their adult feelings, parents may also hope to spare children from having to confront the painful reality of their sibling's disability. This protection may, however, only serve to heighten the mystery of the child's autism. As I discussed in Chapter 2, the explanations siblings invent for their brother's or sister's behavior can be far more frightening than the realities of the disorder. It is therefore important that parents provide age-appropriate explanations and ensure that siblings have facts, and not fantasy, around which to respond to the disability. This information may also help children understand why the sibling with autism needs extra parental attention, and ease some of the jealous or resentful feelings that almost inevitably follow when a child sees a parent's attention being directed more to another child than to himself. Once again, the truth is healthier than a fantasy your child might create to explain why you spend more time with his sister with autism than you do with him.

Between Husband and Wife

Good communication in a family has to happen between husband and wife as well as between parent and child. What happens between parents matters not only to those two adults, but to the children as well. A father confided in me that he was struggling with feelings of anger and grief about his young son's autism. He felt unable to share these feelings with his wife, because he knew how upset she was over their son's diagnosis. As her husband he believed he needed to be strong and protect her from his sorrow. Ironically, a few weeks before, his wife had told me how upset she was by her husband's apparent lack of distress about their son. She could not understand why he did not seem to care very much about the boy's problems. His being unemotional made her feel all the worse, because she felt all alone with her sadness. In this particular case, a bit of encouragement to the father to share some of his feelings with his wife allowed them both to feel better. He realized that his wife respected his feelings of sorrow, and she discovered she was not alone in her pain. This improvement in their own communication allowed them both to be more open with their eight-year-old daughter, who was going through her own process of adjustment to her brother's disability. None of us stands alone in a family.

Learning to communicate with a spouse takes practice, effort, and trust. Some couples do very well at this, but some may need outside help to get the process going. Consulting a professional therapist or religious advisor with counseling skills is a wise course of action if a marriage is especially unhappy.

Between Children

When one child has autism, the verbal communication between siblings may be very limited. This will be especially true if the child with autism also has mental retardation, as we saw in the case of Joe Martin that opened this chapter. Joe lacked much of the vocabulary and sentence structure, as well as the ability to understand, needed to take part in the interpersonal complexities of conversation. Under these conditions, words will be of limited value, and the child with autism will communicate mainly through behavior. A child with autism who is of normal intelligence might have a full vocabulary and be able to generate grammatically correct sentences, but still not be able to understand and express emotional reactions. Thus, regardless of the intellectual functioning level of the child with autism, the communication between children will be improved if parents can be sensitive to the frustration of the normally developing child in trying to understand the child with autism, and can provide the necessary support to help the process move forward.

When the children are young, parents will have to actively structure much of this communication. You can attempt to translate the behavior of the child with autism for his sister. For example, "He ignores you because he doesn't know how to play," or "Tantrums are the only way John knows how to say 'no.'" As she gets older, the normally developing child will learn to "read" her brother's behavior and to interpret his language. A higher functioning child with autism may become quite effective at conversing about factual matters, but be more limited in sharing feelings. The sibling should still be encouraged to express her feelings, both to the child with autism and to her parents. Over time the child with autism may become more aware of other people's feelings, and his siblings can help him with that learning.

Your child with autism will have great difficulty understanding his sibling. As a result he will fail to follow instructions, not recognize that his behavior is upsetting, and largely ignore the sibling. This ignoring, or even active avoidance, can be perplexing and very upsetting to a sibling who yearns for a playmate. Both of your children will need your help in getting beyond these barriers. Chapter 5 discusses some specific things you can do to help the sibling establish communication through play with the child with autism.

Skills for Communicating

Once parents have decided to share information about autism with siblings, they can work toward building an atmosphere which encourages openness. The most basic skill to effective communication between parent and child is good listening. That is more difficult than it may seem, because most of the time when we have a conversation we are only half listening to the other person. We may be devoting the rest of our attention to scrambling ahead in the discussion to think about what we will say next, or how to solve the other person's problem.

Although teaching your child how to solve problems is important, many times simply hearing her out is more important. You may have found in your own experience that as we talk about our problems with a good listener, often we will come up with our own solution. Being able to "own" the solution to our problems is usually more satisfying than having someone else solve them. As a result, listening should usually take precedence over problem solving. For example, your child might come to you concerned because she wants to invite a friend over and wonders how that child will feel about her brother with autism. Your first response should be to give her a chance to talk it out while you listen carefully to her. If your daughter cannot figure out her own answers, or if the two of you need to arrive at a joint solution, that can wait until you have talked through the problem. Don't rush to the end before you explore the middle. The first step in effective communication with your child is to learn how to listen well. This takes practice.

Listening does not always involve words. Sometimes children communicate with their behavior. Parents need to be attuned to what children do not say, as well as what they do. Changes in behavior can be important. The chatty child who has grown silent, the cheerful child who seems sad, or the cooperative child who becomes defiant, each may be attempting to communicate. The child who seems to be in special need of attention, who is clinging and needy, or who avoids his parents and turns away from their affection, may be saying without words that he is distressed. Be attuned to your child's behavior as well as his words.

Rule 1: The Right Place. One essential of good listening is to be certain the circumstances are right. Unless it is an emergency, it is best not to have an important discussion until you have the time and can focus on your child. But, if you cannot respond right away, you need to be sure to set a time for sharing. For example, if a child mentions a problem while you are hurrying to get everyone out the door and off to school, it may not be possible to stop for an extended conversation. But, you can pause at least briefly, make eye contact, perhaps touch the child, and say something like, "No time to talk now. Let's do it when you get home." Similarly, if you wish to initiate a discussion with your child you need to find a time which is going to be conducive to discussion. A child who is eager to go outside and play soccer with her friends will probably not be very receptive to an extended conversation that keeps her from her play. To minimize that kind of problem you might plan a private time together or, if it is an issue that involves the whole family, call a family meeting for the purpose of sharing your concern.

Rule 2: Feedback and Affirmation. Another aspect of effective communication is checking to be sure you understand what your child is saying, and letting her know you understand. That can be done by occasionally making comments such as, "I think I know how you feel" or "uh huh" or "That made you mad." If you are not certain what your child means, you might try saying something like, "I want to be sure I follow what you're saying. If I understand you, it makes you really sad when your brother can't play with you like other kids do." That process of reflecting feelings and confirming for your child that you are listening carefully can be very helpful in building an atmosphere in which your child feels that you truly wish to understand her. Sometimes repeating her feelings back to her may help her clarify to herself what she is feeling. We have probably all had the experience of realizing that things sound different when we say them out loud rather than just thinking them to ourselves.

I think it is important not to assume you know what another person means when she speaks. I try to listen closely, and if I do not know exactly what she means, I ask her to help me understand. For example, sometimes we use words differently. My "angry" may be your "boiling mad," and my "happy" may be your "sky high." One mother I know kept using the word "tense" when I would have said "angry." When I asked her what she meant by tense, the experience she described fit very closely what I would mean by "angry," although she focused more on her physical sensations of anger and I might have attended more to the angry thoughts. I would not have known for sure what she meant by "tense" if I had not asked her.

Rule 3: Being Open about Your Own Feelings. Communication is a two-way street. In addition to being a good listener, it is important to share your own feelings and thoughts. That means modeling for your child honesty of communication, and sharing information and feelings appropriate to her age. We need to be able to tell other people what we like about them as well as what bothers us about what they do. Some people find it easier to share loving feelings than angry ones, while for others it may be easier to voice anger than love. A healthy balance of communication is important. Children need to know they are loved and cherished; they also need to know what they do that troubles us. Sharing negative and positive emotions in a constructive way is a valuable parenting skill.

Often we state our distress about what a child is doing by speaking harshly or angrily. This is usually based on the assumption that the child knows what he is doing and wishes to upset us. Although that may sometimes be true, frequently a child does not know he is upsetting us unless we tell him so. In addition, children often do things without being aware of their effect. A very young child may say, "Don't be messy," at the same time he smears a puddle of milk on the table. His words and thoughts do not always control his behavior. Even older children often fail to reflect before they act. A child may need constructive feedback about a behavior in order to change it. However, when we vent strong anger rather than sharing more modulated feelings, it becomes hard for a child to hear us, and perhaps hard to make a change without losing face. As a result, it is best when our feedback is clear, but the effect is not overwhelming to the child.

Consider this example of sharing negative feelings with a child. Mr. R. is upset with his older son. The boy left his model building equipment scattered in the living room when he went out to play, and his younger sister, who has autism, found the equipment and cut herself on a sharp edge. She then became very agitated and was hard to calm.

Mr. R. is at a choice point for communication when he hears the back door close and knows his son has just returned home. Let us examine two possible responses. In the first scene, as his son walks in, Mr. R. gets up and yells at him, "You left your model building equipment all over the place. Your sister cut herself, and then she had a tantrum and I had a terrible time getting her settled down. Why can't you be more responsible?" That may be an honest sharing of feelings, but it is almost certain to leave everyone more upset without solving the problem.

In the alternative scene, Mr. R. says as the boy walks in, "Son, we have a problem we need to solve. I know sometimes you get so excited that you forget to put your things away before you go outside to be with your friends. It's tough to remember to be neat when you feel so happy. But, it makes my day a lot tougher when you leave your gear around and your sister hurts herself and has one of her tantrums. We need to figure out how you can learn to be more careful with your things." In this second scene the father shares his sense of frustration, but makes the assumption that his son needs help learning to be neat, rather than that he is irresponsible. The next step would be to problem solve with his son about their mutual problem.

Table 1
RULES FOR FAMILY MEETINGS

1. The whole family should be present.

2. The television is turned off and the telephone answering machine is turned on.

3. No company.

4. Everyone who wants to gets a turn to talk.

5. Everyone listens while one person talks.

6. People should do their best to share their thoughts and feelings.

7. It is not fair to make fun of someone else's thoughts and feelings.

8. If the family cannot agree, parents have the final word.

The problem solving would include agreeing on an appropriate set of consequences. For example, the father might offer to buy his son a new model kit if the son keeps his equipment in a safe place for the next couple of weeks. However, if he is not careful with the gear, the equipment might be taken away for a couple of days.

Rule 4: Accepting the Other Person's Feelings. We may not always agree with one another, but it is important to respect the legitimacy of one another's feelings. If your daughter shares with you her anger about the time you spend with her brother, it is important to be open to her feelings and validate them as normal and understandable. If you get angry and defensive when she shares these feelings, it will probably close off lines of communication. Do your best to put yourself in your child's shoes, and listen respectfully to her feelings. For example, you can say that you might feel the same if you were in her spot or reflect to her that you understand how very upset she feels. If you can do that, it is likely that she will go on to share even more with you. The more fully you have heard your daughter's feelings, the more likely you are to be able to help her.

Acknowledging that feelings are legitimate does not mean that it is OK for a child to act on them. Your daughter has to learn to talk about what she feels rather than to vent the emotions directly. For example, she should tell you she is angry rather than tormenting her brother. It will take time and patience on your part to help your child achieve this goal.

Although some children respond well to parents' efforts at communicating, some do not. If you are unable to reach your child in spite of your best efforts, or if your child's behaviors are especially troubling, you may want to consider the help of a professional therapist. For example, a sister who consistently shuns her brother with autism, or who disobeys important family rules, may need outside help. Similarly, a child who is chronically angry and repeatedly says such things as that she wishes her brother were dead or that he was in a mental hospital may need more help than you alone can give her.

Family Conferences

Communication does not always happen one-on-one. As we saw in the case of the Martin family that opened this chapter, it can be helpful to bring the entire family together to share information or to problem solve when an issue comes up that may touch everyone's life. This can concern the child with autism or any other issue. A family meeting can be called by any member of the family, parent or child. Although Rosemary and Dan Martin had called the meeting discussed in the beginning of this chapter, any of the children were also welcome to request such a meeting.

These family meetings should be viewed as a special time. There should be family rules such as those shown in Table 1. At these meetings, parents can share with children important information, ask their opinions about impending family decisions, or jointly make plans for family events. People can also brainstorm about solutions to family problems (Forgatch & Patterson, 1989). This was the technique used by the Martin family to plan their celebration of Joe's graduation from school. As the first step, everyone just tossed out ideas. It might be something as impossible as Rich's suggestion of a trip around the world, or as practical as Kathy's idea of a trip to Washington, DC.

After they had made up a list of possibilities, some wild and some practical, the Martin family discussed the list and finally decided that Joe's idea of going camping was the best of all. Notice that the Martins all tried not to make fun of each other's ideas. Even when Rich mentioned the trip around the world, it was written down on the list as one possibility. People who do research on brainstorming tell us it is important not to judge the merits of any idea too soon or it will make it harder for people to feel free to make their contributions. The sorting out of possible and impossible solutions happens after the brainstorming is finished. Family brainstorming is a chance to let your imagination run loose for a while.

Closing Comments

In sum, communication is not a one-time event. It is an on-going process that shifts and changes with the ages of the children and needs of the family. Sometimes you will do a wonderful job of communicating, and sometimes you may feel disappointed that you did not listen as well as you might have, or did not share as openly as you wish you could. That's OK. We all have our stronger and weaker moments. What matters is that the overall atmosphere in your family is one in which people are all working to understand one another's experiences and jointly solve problems. Children can be very forgiving of mistakes when they know their parents are trying hard to do the right thing. Besides, there is not a parent in all of written history who did not make at least a few mistakes in child rearing!

PARENTS SPEAK

I firmly believe that if Tommy had been born without autism my children would have had a vastly different childhood. Be that as it may, the suggestion I have for other parents is to be there for them and talk to them openly about their feelings, whether bad or good, concerning the autistic sibling. We as parents have shared all of our trials and tribulations concerning Tommy with our other children. We have encouraged them to voice their opinions when they wanted to. This in turn has made them feel a very important part of Tommy's life and has helped to ease the stress in many situations.

I believe that as long as a family is open and honest with each other they can get through almost any situation. Tommy is the prime topic of conversation in our home and no matter how the children are feeling about him that day, they express those feelings. Sometimes the problem isn't completely resolved, but at least they

know we are there to listen and try to help whenever
we can.

We went through a hard time with our oldest boy,
Martin, a couple of years ago when he was 13. Martin
had always been a sunny, cheerful boy who was helpful
with his younger sister Emma, who has autism. All of a
sudden Martin went from being social, cheerful, and
helpful to a sad boy who spent most of his time in his
room. When I would ask him what was wrong he would
just get sullen and go to his room. My wife and I were
at our wit's end. Finally, one day I sat him down and
told him we had to talk. I told him his sadness was tearing me apart and I needed to do something to help
him. Finally, very reluctantly he began to admit that he
had heard my wife and me fighting recently about what
to do for Emma who was having some severe behavior
problems. I realized that by trying to protect Martin, we
had just left him with half truths about what was going
on. When we sat down as a family and talked, it
seemed to help him a lot. My wife and I also realized
how much the situation was bothering us and that we
had to do something to resolve it. We ended up going
for some counseling with a psychologist who helped us
a lot.

I have had many problems with my older boy. He
seems to have resented his sister since the day we
brought her home, and when we found out she had

autism and needed a lot of special care, things went from bad to worse. Then, my husband left me a few years ago, and my son has just never gotten over that. I went to a psychologist, and my son and I had some family sessions together. That has helped some. I have learned to be more honest with him, and he has expressed some of his feelings. I also learned how to set more limits for him, so he has to tow the line better now. All that helps, but it is not easy, and some days I feel like I am climbing up a mountain too high to walk alone.

I grew up in a family where people didn't talk very much about their feelings. I promised myself it would be different in my own family, and it is. We talk to the kids a lot about what Christopher needs to cope with his autism, and we share our feelings. I think it has made a big difference all around.

I will always be grateful to my parents for how they talked to me when I was kid. They told me about my brother's autism, and they seemed to be able to understand when I teased him or pushed him around a little. I mean they didn't say it was OK, but they didn't do a real guilt trip either. They would punish me the same way my best friend got punished when he would tease his little sister. No more, and no less. Plus, they would help me find things I could do that would give me a way to play with my brother. It wasn't ideal, and I think they made mistakes like all parents do, but I always knew they would listen to me and try to be fair. I appreciate that all the more now that I'm grown and know how hard it must have been on them raising the two of us and him having autism.

4

THE BALANCING ACT: Finding Time for Family, Work, and Yourself

The Gonzalez Family

Maria Gonzalez felt like she was doing 100 things at once. Pack the lunches, get the cereal on the table, find the baby's teddy so he would stop whining and tugging at her leg, call upstairs to remind her older girl to take the books for the school library drive. It was like a whirlwind every morning, getting the kids off to school, and dropping the baby at her mother's before Maria drove herself to work. Carlos Sr. left early for work, and missed this morning madness, but he got home before her, and was the one who met their son C. J., when he got off the bus from school. C. J. was nine years old and had been in special classes since he was three years old and first diagnosed with autism. Thank heavens for the school. C. J. was doing well, and now spent two hours every day in a regular class and the rest in a special education classroom. Next year they were going to try including him even more in a regular classroom. C. J. was bright, and he was doing fine academically, but his social skills and emotional control were still a problem and he needed a lot of support learning how to get along with other kids. Maria or Carlos had to spend time with him every night, helping him organize his work, or recover from something that upset him.

Driving to work through the freeway traffic, Maria wondered how they all managed as well as they did. Sometimes she felt like she was stretched so thin she might snap. Three kids and a full-time job were just too much. Her oldest daughter, Natalia, was a big help, but Maria worried that with C. J. needing so much extra help, and four-year-old Gus always under foot, she relied too much on Natalia. Natalia had been upset the night before, crying because Maria could not come to a special program at the school Thursday night. There was a parent meeting at C. J.'s school, and Maria felt she must be there. Natalia had wept and protested that nothing she did was as important as what C. J. did. It made Maria feel terrible, and she did not know what to do to help Natalia understand how much she loved her.

It wasn't just her relationship with Natalia that worried her. She had so little time with her husband. Often by the time they fell in bed at night, they were both too tired to talk, much less to make love, or even to cuddle and feel close to each other. Maria remembered with a sigh what a wonderful, tender man Carlos was, and she felt a loneliness for him.

The parking lot loomed ahead of her. Time to switch channels and concentrate on her job. She liked work and enjoyed the people she worked with. Sometimes the office felt like the only place where she had any private time at all. How wonderful to walk in to her office, take a cup of coffee, close the door, and finally be surrounded by silence for a few minutes before the phone rang.

Introduction

Many of the demands faced by Maria Gonzalez are part of life in any family, regardless of whether there is a child with autism. Family life is a balancing act. Parents are often struggling to meet the needs of their children, their partner, and themselves. If both parents work, the demands are even more intense because all of the household chores must be addressed as well as the responsibilities from work. These stresses are inherent in family life as we know it in western culture. If there is a child with autism, the responsibilities can be further heightened by that child's special needs. These added needs of the child with autism can be so intense as to make it impossible for a woman to work outside the home, while the father works more hours to make up for the income lost when his wife does not work (Alessandri, 1992).

As we saw in the episode that opened this chapter, Maria Gonzalez struggled to meet the many competing demands that faced her. Mother, wife, daughter, employee, each of these roles pressed on her, often at the same time. Each was valid, and each important. How to choose? Was it more important to go to parents' night at C. J.'s school or the performance at Natalia's school? What she really wanted to do was stay home and put her feet up for the evening!

Research suggests that mothers spend more time with a child with a disability than with a normally developing child (McHale & V. Harris, 1992). This difference in attention can lead to jealous feelings on the part of other children in the family. It is probably not simply the amount of time spent with them that makes the most difference to other children in the family, but what they believe this difference means. If the normally developing children feel that their parents love the child with autism more than themselves, that will probably have a more negative impact than if they are able to understand the reason for the difference in attention. Once again this argues for the importance of good communication in the family.

Older children sometimes tell me that they know how hard it is for their mother and father to do everything that has to be done for a sibling with autism, and they understand why that child gets more attention. However, even the most understanding of siblings is likely to encounter some episodes when this difference in attention seems very unfair. We saw this in the case of the Gonzalez family, when Natalia felt her mother's attention to C. J. was depriving her of the time she needed.

There are no perfect solutions to the demands on parents for time and resources. It is inevitable that you will have to make choices, and sometimes one or more members of your family will be disappointed by the outcome. That happens in every family. But, with planning it may be possible to reduce the disappointments, and with effective communication it may be possible to decrease the upset feelings when things do not work out as your child had hoped they might.

You Love Her More

Children are very alert to differences in how they are treated. Such differences in treatment are inevitable, and sometimes they are even desirable, but they can form the basis for resentment and disappointment. We typically give different privileges, bed times, allowances, and responsibilities to children at different ages. If you have two children, your treatment of each is based on age, maturity, and need. These decisions seem rational and wise to you, but may seem less fair to your child who sees herself as receiving the smaller portion of privileges, even if she is younger than her brother who has been granted more age-appropriate freedom. However, your child can be helped to understand that some privileges are granted not because one child is loved more than the other, but because with age comes increasing freedom as well as increasing responsibility. Even though they may protest a bit, children can usually understand the justice in this formula as long as they find that they too receive their fair share as they grow up, and as long as they feel loved and valued by their parents.

Differences in privileges based on age may be relatively easy to explain to your child. It is harder to explain to children, especially when they are young, why one sibling receives the preponderance of parental attention because he has autism. Natalia Gonzalez's resentment that her parents were going to C. J.'s school meeting instead of hers is very understandable. She may have been correct in her judgment that she was not getting her share of parental attention, although that lack of equity was not due to a lack of love on her parents' part. To the contrary, Maria valued Natalia as a dear child and her only daughter. She also very much appreciated Natalia as her strongest helper at home. Nonetheless, Maria and Carlos Sr. had not worked out a balance of attention that would help Natalia feel she was getting her fair share of their time. Potential solutions to this kind of dilemma are considered in this chapter.

Together or Apart?

How do you feel about doing things as a family? Many parents believe that family activities should always be shared as a family unit. If they are going to the museum, the whole family should go, and if they are going to one child's Little League baseball game, everyone else should come along. When there is a child with autism, parents may feel especially strongly that this child should always be included in family events. They want to make it clear that the youngster is a full member of the family and the community, and not someone to be left home with a babysitter while the rest of the family has a good time.

Although I respect the idea that everyone in the family should share family events, I believe it is important to think flexibly about who should be included in an event. If your older child has a concert, and your younger child with autism is not able to sit quietly through the music, I believe it is usually more important for parents to go to the concert by themselves than it is to include the child with autism and risk disrupting an important moment for the older child. Every child needs a chance to shine, and sometimes a sibling with autism can cast a shadow that never allows another child to be the center of attention. It is not only OK, it is probably very important to give each child some separate time with mother, with father, and with both parents together. That is true in all families, not just those where a child has autism. Perhaps you have some fond memories from your own childhood of a special event where you were the center of your parents' attention. You will want to give your own child similar memories for the years ahead.

Time spent together need not be lengthy, or occur every day with each parent, or revolve around a special event. But at least several times a week, each child should know that he has the opportunity to spend some private time with Mother or Father. During that time a parent should do her best to focus on that child. For example, a father might take his daughter with him to pick up a tool at the hardware store on Saturday morning. During the drive over and back he would make her the focus of his attention, using the kinds of communication skills discussed in Chapter 3. During this same interval his wife might be going to the dry cleaner, taking along their young son with autism.

One of the things the Gonzalez family decided to do to help make sure they were touching base with the children each day was to take turns putting the younger children to bed and to spend time with Natalia before she went upstairs on her own at bed time. One night Carlos would work with C. J., talking with him about the day just passed and planning tomorrow's routine, while Maria tucked Gus into bed, taking 10 or 15 minutes to talk with him, sing to him, and cuddle him. Later in the evening when it was Natalia's bedtime, one of her parents would sit in the kitchen with her while she had her night-time snack. This was a time for sharing. By doing this consistently every night, they found they had at least a few minutes a day of private time with each child. This focused attention helped them both be more alert to potential problems, and the children valued knowing they each would have some undivided parental attention each day.

Another approach Maria and Carlos might have taken would be to carve out a longer period of time a few days a week, or to have a special shared activity such as playing tennis together each Saturday morning or going for a long walk on Sunday afternoon.

After they had their schedule for the children in place, Maria insisted that she and Carlos needed to make a plan for themselves. Maria knew that she needed to have some private time with Carlos if she were going to sustain the energy she needed for the children. So, they asked four people, Maria's mother, her aunt, Carlos's younger brother, and a good friend from high school, to each help them out one Saturday night a month. With these four helpers, each of whom understood C.J.'s special needs, Maria and Carlos were able to look forward to one evening a week that belonged to them. Just knowing that they had this time to look forward to made it easier to put up with the hassles of the week. If they had not been able to turn to friends and family, the Gonzalezes would have been wise to consider professional respite care from a state or professional agency, support from church members, or child care help from special education students from a nearby college or university to meet their need for private time.

Being Together

It is important for a child to have special time with a parent, but it is also important to be together as a family. Part of what it means to be a family is to share things: to make group decisions about shared activities, to go places together, to have family jokes, and family fun. It is important for your normally developing children to understand that your child with autism is part of that, just as they need to understand that sometimes they will do things separately from the child with autism.

Parents need to be alert for feelings of embarrassment by a sibling who does not want to be seen in public with her brother with autism. She may voice this directly, or she may start to avoid family activities. This may become an issue in preadolescence when children become acutely concerned with how they appear in the eyes of their peer group. These feelings should be listened to and respected as an expression of the child's experience. Her feelings should not be the basis for dropping all family activities, but compromise may be necessary. These feelings of discomfort are not unique to the sibling of a child with autism. Many adolescents want to "disown" their family and may lay down strict rules to their parents about how they are to be treated in public. For example, a teenager may ask his parents not to hug him in public, or comb his hair, or use a family nickname. Similarly, parents may agree not to bring a difficult-to-manage child with autism to an important event for the teenager, but rather focus their family time on activities of a more private nature such as riding bikes in the country or a camping trip. In this way one can protect the feelings of the teenager and still enjoy some shared times.

Finding activities that can be shared by the child with autism can sometimes be a challenge. Perhaps it is helpful to understand that the skills necessary for this kind of sharing can be mastered over time just as other skills, like speech or self-help skills, are gradually learned and made more complex. Your child's teacher can be a valuable consultant in identifying activities within the capacity of your child and in helping create programs to enable your child to learn the skills.

Examples of shared family activities which can be performed very competently by many people with autism are jogging, bowling, or bike riding. Shopping at the mall, preparing a special meal, or going to a movie may also be shared events. I know a family whose adolescent son with autism is fascinated by maps. He is the navigator on family trips, telling the driver when to turn, and warning the passengers to be alert to upcoming scenic spots from the guidebook. This role keeps him happy and makes him an integral part of family trips. It may take the person with autism longer to master the basic skills of an activity, but if one begins with modest goals and gradually builds to broader objectives, it is reasonable to expect that many young persons with autism could go on a family bike trip or go jogging with a parent or sibling each morning.

Similarly, if your child with autism has a hard time tolerating a family trip to the shopping mall, you may have to gradually build his tolerance for the experience. This can mean going only for a brief time, and slowly increasing the amount of time spent. It can also mean going at quiet times when there are fewer people and less noise and confusion. Initially trips may need to include two adults with two cars, so one person can make a graceful exit with the child with autism, while the other completes the chores at the shopping mall. A ten-minute trip can grow each month to be a bit longer, until your child with autism is able to tolerate a full trip and to enjoy the experience. Even when a child resists every new activity, it is important for parents to persist in introducing new things to do. People with autism need to learn to tolerate change if they are to function effectively in the world, and learning to manage the stress of change is therefore an important lesson of childhood.

Private Space

It is important to share time together, but it is also important that everyone in the family have time to be separate. Time alone may be the hardest commodity to come by in a family, and it may take a lot of planning to achieve the goal. However, parents as a couple, and individually, need time away from their children. You need time to renew yourself, time to enjoy your spouse, and time to feel a sense of yourself as a separate person. This is not simply self-indulgence. It seems to be important to good mental health that persons in our society have the opportunity both to feel part of a unit and to experience themselves as separate people. Although there are individual differences and cultural differences in how much private time we need, most persons who grow up in Western society have learned to treasure a certain amount of separateness.

Children, too, need some private time. Time for their own hobbies, to watch the clouds float by, or to ride their bike to a favorite thinking place. That leisure is one of the things many of us treasure about our childhood memories. Having a sibling with autism may make that private time a little harder to come by, unless parents are very sensitive to protecting their child from excessive demands. Childcare and household chores should not be so extensive that your child is denied free time.

It is important that children learn to carry their share of family responsibilities, including spending time with their brother or sister with autism, but responsibilities should not overpower the time a child needs to pursue his or her own life. Some children are so helpful to parents that it may be difficult to recognize that they have taken on too much responsibility and are paying the price by giving away some of their own childhood. The child who comes home from school to a load of chores and homework will have little opportunity to savor the freedom of childhood. This was in danger of happening to Natalia Gonzalez until her parents recognized the pattern and made some changes in their routine.

As part of a child's right to privacy, parents should try to provide physical boundaries for the space, possessions, and activities of the normally developing child. Ideally this would mean giving each of your children a bedroom of their own, with a lock on the door if necessary. If that degree of privacy is not possible, and the room is shared with the child with autism, the siblings need some secure space. For example, a lock might be put on a closet, drawer, or foot locker where prized possessions can be stored without fear of damage by the child with autism. If your child with autism does damage a sibling's belongings, you should respond with empathy to the sibling's anger, sadness, or frustration. You can do this by listening to your child's distress and conveying your understanding of his feelings. Your response should not stop here. When possible, the item should be replaced. To the extent that it is feasible, your child with autism should also receive some consequence for the destruction, and be taught how to be more responsible. For example, he might have to spend time alone in his room (time out) and clean up the mess he made in his brother's room. The specific consequence will vary with the functioning level of your child with autism. Similarly, if your child with autism always intrudes on his sibling's activities, you should either provide a separate play area or supervise the child in a different activity.

Everyone Contributes to a Family

I have focused a lot in this book on protecting children from becoming auxiliary parents with excessive responsibilities for their brother or sister with autism. The sibling should not have an adult disciplinary role for the child with autism or full-time childcare responsibilities after school or on weekends. Although they might issue mild reprimands (e.g., "stop tearing up the paper") or suggest alternative activities (e.g., "go play with your puzzles"), they would not be expected to put a child in time out or require him to clean up a mess. Nor should they be responsible for making decisions about the welfare of your child with autism.

Although children should be buffered from adult roles, they are part of the family and should carry their own weight. Even young children can do little chores like putting their dishes in the dishwasher. Older children can make greater contributions such as clearing the entire table, loading the dishwasher, and putting the clean dishes away. They can also spend a brief period of time each day with their brother or sister with autism. If your child does not pose a management problem, an adolescent sibling could babysit in the evening or on a weekend.

Your child with autism should also start to contribute to the family at an early age. This may begin with putting her plastic cup on the counter after dinner, and gradually evolve to clearing the table, folding laundry, mowing the lawn, and so forth. Like your other children, she will need these skills in adult life, and she will be contributing to the entire family as she learns them. The other children in the family are less likely to resent her if she, too, has chores.

Using Resources

Perhaps as you have been reading this chapter you have wondered how it is possible for a person to do all the things I have described. Being able to spend time with each child, with your spouse, and by yourself can take a lot of juggling. Parents cannot always meet these needs by themselves, and single parents and parents with many children may find themselves overwhelmed unless they have help.

The parents of a child with autism should draw on every resource they can identify to give themselves extra help. You can start close to home, with relatives who might lend a hand. An aunt or uncle, grandparent, or cousin might be willing to stay with one or more of your children for a scheduled time each week or each month. Sometimes friends or neighbors will do the same. Many people find members of their church or synagogue are happy to help out with childcare as well. These sitters will need a chance to get to know your child while you are present so they can feel at ease when you are away. Many parents whom I know invite a sitter over a couple of times to care for the child while they are home. This gives them a chance to check out the sitter and to train that person in working with their child.

Other parents of children with autism may be an especially useful resource. You could trade children for a day or a weekend, and know that someone who really understands your child is in charge. These families are also likely to have homes that are well "child proofed." Although this arrangement is hectic when you have the children, it is great when you are the one to get away!

Your emotional well-being is at stake, so do not be shy about asking other people to lend a hand. It makes people feel good and helps build a broad sense of community and belonging when we help each other. I think the idea of self-sufficiency and rugged individualism that is so cherished by many people in Western culture, when carried to an extreme, tends to undermine the sense of social connection so essential to a feeling of being part of a community. When we are allowed to give to one another, we build our community and contribute to a common good. So, calling on family and friends to lend a hand not only enhances the welfare of your family, it is good for the community as a whole!

Psychologists refer to family and friends as a person's informal support network. The more people you have available in your network to call on for help, the better your life is likely to be. It is important to build this informal network. It helps reduce your vulnerability to feelings of sadness and isolation when there are many hands to help out. It is better to have several helpers rather than only one or two, because there is a better chance there will always be someone available when you need assistance, and no one will get burned out from too much use. So, even if your mother says she wants to do it all, reach out to others as well. Similarly, an extended social network gives your other children many people they can turn to for help.

It is also important to call on your formal support network. These are the professionals in the community who provide services for persons with autism. For example, respite services can be a help to the whole family. In-home respite care involves having a trained person come into your home to provide care for your child with autism. Out-of-home respite can entail short-term placement of your child with autism in the home of a respite worker or a group home set up for short-term visits. For example, if a parent needs to have surgery, or if a family needs to go away, out-of-home respite would provide a few days of childcare. Some people are shy about asking for this help. I believe you should ask for everything you need. The more help you have in raising your child with autism, the better the job you can probably do for your child, your family, and for yourself. People who are chronically exhausted do not usually do as good a job of parenting as they could if they were rested. Your local autism society chapter should be able to help you find agencies that provide respite care. These respite services are often paid for in whole or in part by your state or county government, but you will need to register with a state agency and ask for the help. There usually is a waiting list for services unless a family is in an emergency situation.

Sometimes there are difficulties in calling on family members to help out. For example, my colleagues and I did some research a few years ago which showed that grandparents tended to underestimate the seriousness of the impact of a child's autism on the family (Harris, Handleman, & Palmer, 1985). Perhaps because they do not usually live with the child, they may not understand just how hard it is to give the child everything he needs. It may also be that their own adult children have not shared with the grandparents how difficult things can be for them. Just as your children wish to protect you from their feelings, so, too, you may be trying to protect your own parents. However, most parents with whom we have worked tell us that after they have shared their concerns with their own parents, these grandparents can become an important source of support.

It is helpful if you can be direct with your friends or relatives about what you and your family need. If your Aunt Lucy invites the whole clan for Thanksgiving, and the noise and confusion is too upsetting for your four-year-old with autism, you need to tell Aunt Lucy that. Maybe you can drop by for a short visit; maybe several people can take turns playing with your son in a quiet room, while others are part of the party; or maybe it will be easier to stay home on Thanksgiving, inviting just a few people to join you, and visit with your aunt on a quieter day. Other people may not know what you, your son, and the rest of the family need until you tell them. Creating an atmosphere where your child with autism is comfortable should help to ensure the other children will have fun as well.

Parent Support Groups

Parent support groups can help you learn to respond to the needs of your child with autism and to your family as a whole. This is an opportunity to share feelings, concerns, and coping responses. It can be comforting to realize the extent to which others share your experiences and understand what you are feeling. Other people's solutions may serve as guides to your own resolution of a problem. Sometimes other families may provide tangible support such as joining together to take all of the children on an outing, or sharing child care.

Parents talk about many things in these support groups. Frequently the topics under discussion include the needs of siblings. Parents may share "guilty" feelings for not being more available to their other children, concern about how to explain autism to a young child, or fears about conceiving another child with autism. If you are looking for a good forum to explore your feelings and find emotional support from other people who will understand your experiences, a group like this can be a good bet. Some schools for children with autism offer parent support groups, and your local autism society chapter may also be able to help you find this kind of support.

Sibling Support Groups

Support groups are not limited to parents. Siblings value the experience as well. Sibling groups can give children an opportunity to talk about feelings such as their anger at peers for rejecting a brother or sister with autism; fear of "inheriting" autism; jealousy; and resentment of the need to compete for parental attention. Sometimes it is easier to voice these feelings outside of the family, and other children can help to affirm the acceptable nature of uncomfortable emotions.

Unlike our parent support groups, where the participants set the agenda, in our sibling groups we have a planned sequence that extends across several weeks. These groups may consist of about half a dozen children of relatively close ages, such as 7 to 12 years. The sessions are a combination of a group activity, group discussion, and snack time. The children may create a group drawing to illustrate the concept of individual differences in development, dictate to the adult leader a list of important questions about autism, or discuss some of their feelings about their brother or sister. We have found some of the activities in psychologist Debra Lobato's (1990) book about sibling groups very helpful in facilitating discussion among children.

The first session always includes a brief meeting with parents and children together to discuss the plans for the group and lay the groundwork of confidentiality. At the final meeting we again include a session with parents. As part of this discussion the group leaders review a list of items the children identified as important for parents to know. This enables the children to share concerns as a group and allows parents to follow up on topics they wish to pursue at home. Although the specific format of the group will vary with the ages of the children, these kinds of activities can be quite helpful. Your child's teacher or your local autism society chapter may be able to help you find a sibling group. Be certain it is run by someone with appropriate credentials such as a school psychologist, clinical psychologist, or social worker.

Closing Comments

Living in a family is one of the most difficult things we do. There are so many competing needs that must be met, and so little time to do so. Autism is not the only source of family stress, but if you have a child with autism, the demands of family life may be even more intense because that youngster needs so much extra help to meet his potential. The stress created by those demands can be a breeding ground for anxiety, tension, sadness, jealousy, and other painful emotions on the part of any family member.

Meeting the many demands of family life, and helping each family member develop a fulfilling life, may hinge in part on being able to draw on the resources around you. It makes good sense to ask family, friends, and professionals to contribute what they can to helping your family thrive. If you are a single parent, or a couple raising your children far from your own families, you may need to make an extra effort to reach out to your friends in the community. The more helpers you have, the better.

Fortunately, although family life is demanding, it can also be profoundly rewarding, and your children may emerge as richer adults for having been part of a family that included a youngster with autism.

PARENTS SPEAK

In keeping with this idea of occupying Matt's time, we have encouraged him to be independent and responsible around the house. He can cook, set the table, load the dishwasher, bring out the trash, etc. He has also developed interests in coloring, reading, arts and crafts, and helping his dad paint and work with tools on various home projects.

I sometimes think back to that powerfully energetic toddler. What I see today is an eight-year-old boy who is constructively busy most of the time, and happy being so. This has allowed me more time with my daughter, and a more relaxed and happy family life in general.

In giving direction to Matt's life, we have managed to take control of ours. When I now take some time for myself, I find it is not motivated by a desperate need, but by more of a healthy desire.

I know I am not an expert at managing the complex balancing act within our family. I hope I am doing a decent job, but sometimes I'm not so sure. Unfortunately, parents of autistic children aren't given any special graces to deal with these circumstances. We are just ordinary people in very extraordinary situations.

I really feel there is a part of your life you must neglect to keep up with the other demands. In my case I have never worked outside the home since Tommy's problems began. Some people may be able to do this, but I always felt I could not give my all to both at the same time.

It was hard for me at first, but I have finally started to ask other people for help. We applied to a local agency for respite care. We get 20 hours a month and that has made a big difference for all of us. My husband and I make it a point to go out together at least once a week, even if it is just for a movie.

One of the hardest things for me was letting my family know that I needed more help from them. My mom was great once I asked her. She said I always seemed to have everything under control and she didn't want to intrude. Once I told her I could use the help, she was great.

One of the toughest things for me about my son's autism has been how my family has reacted. When my parents heard that Dick had autism they just seemed to disappear. They never offer to sit with him. My sister-in-law asked me to leave Dick at home when they had a family party and invited all the other children. Those things just go right to my heart. So, I don't see much of my family, but it hurts a lot. When we talk in our parent support group about how some people have families who are so great in helping, I just want to cry all over again.

My husband and I have been trying to get together with other parents of children with autism and do things together. Sort of make a new family to help each other. It isn't the same as if my mom did it, but it helps to have friends who care.

When our teenager was 13 he went through a time when he did not want to be seen in public with us. If we went to the mall, he would walk about a dozen paces behind me so that people would not see him with me and think he wasn't "cool." I can understand that. I went through it myself when I was young. What was hard for me was that he especially did not want to be seen with his younger sister who has autism. She can be quite a handful, doing things like dropping to the floor and having a tantrum in the middle of a shopping trip. I wasn't sure if I should insist on her being with us, but I finally realized that if I pushed him very hard it might make more trouble. He was good to his sister at home, and if we were hiking in the woods or some place private, he would take care of her, but put him within 50 yards of another adolescent and it was a different story. That phase passed by the time he was 15, and now he seems very comfortable with us and with her. As I look back, I'm glad his mother and I did not push it too hard, and I'm glad we still managed to find some family things to do that were private enough for my son to be at ease. Growing from boy to young man is tough going.

My seven-year-old daughter who has autism broke one of her brother's favorite toys the other day. He was very upset and wanted me to punish her. At first I thought it wouldn't do any good, but then I realized that even if she didn't learn anything, he would feel that I was standing up for him, and it would make him feel better. So, I sent her to her room.

5

CHILDREN AT PLAY: Helping Children Play Together

The Laurel Family

Nine-year-old Rhona Laurel had a healthy zest for life. She delighted in her swimming prowess, was intensely proud to be allowed to ride her bike over the quiet streets of her neighborhood, and loved to play soccer with her friends on the empty lot at the end of her street. She was a well-liked girl with a number of friends. But at home Rhona was a different child. She played quietly in her room, often closing the door to exclude her younger bother, Nick. Rhona had good reason to seek her privacy. Nick could be destructive, smashing a clay pot Rhona had made in crafts class by casually tossing it on the ground, or pushing her partially assembled puzzle on the floor into a shamble of pieces. When Rhona would approach him to play, he would ignore her or push her away. He had been diagnosed with autism six months earlier, and although his behavior at home was getting better because of the good education he was now receiving, his sister was still very cautious with him, afraid of his tantrums and of his seeming indifference to her.

One night when Mrs. Laurel was tucking Rhona into bed, she asked the little girl if she would like to learn how to play with Nick. Mrs. Laurel said that she understood how unhappy Rhona was about Nick destroying her toys and about not hav-

ing him as a playmate. That day Mrs. Laurel had received a letter from Nick's school saying that they were starting a new project to teach siblings play skills, and wondered if Rhona would like to be a part of the program. Rhona grew very excited and begged her mother to call the school that very minute. Mrs. Laurel laughingly reminded her daughter it was night time and the school was closed, but promised she would call in the morning and tell them Rhona wanted to know more about their project for siblings.

Ted Kelly, Nick's preschool teacher, was delighted with Rhona's interest in play skills. He said Nick was learning a lot about simple play at school and it would be wonderful if Rhona wanted to help him play at home as well. He said he would come to the house and teach Rhona and Mr. and Mrs. Laurel how they could help Nick learn to play.

Rhona was excited about her time with Ted and her brother. She knew she was the star of this very important show, and she was determined to help her brother become a wonderful playmate. Ted suggested they start with a very simple activity, one Nick already knew how to do, so Rhona just had to teach him to play the game with her as he did with a child at school. Ted showed Rhona a few basic teaching skills and her parents watched so they could become her coaches. She learned how to make sure Nick was paying attention to her when she asked him to do something, to model for him how to do it, and to praise him when he got it right. With her mother and father cheering her on and helping her refine her skills, she quickly mastered the basic activities she needed to play with Nick.

Although Rhona still spends most of her time playing with her own friends, she now enjoys spending some time

*each day with her little brother, Nick. They are playing sim-
ple games like catch, and rolling cars, and making animal
sounds. Sometimes Nick acts up a little and Rhona will call
her father or mother to help her, but usually Nick enjoys his
time with his sister, and listens carefully to her directions. He
gets excited when she calls him to play, and Rhona glows
with the pleasure of being his companion at long last.*

Introduction

Rhona's frustration at not being able to play with her
brother is not unusual for siblings of children with autism.
Neither is the pleasure she felt once she mastered some basic
skills and was able to engage Nick in simple play activities. My
own work with young siblings of children with autism has
shown me time and again that many of them can master the
skills they need to play with their brother or sister. Most importantly, this play can become mutually pleasurable for both
children.

If you think that kind of play might be appropriate for
your children, the information in this chapter may be helpful.
I will briefly describe what is known about how siblings can
help children with autism learn to play. I will also discuss
some of the issues involved when children become "teachers."
Then, I will share with you in some detail the procedures my
colleague David Celiberti and I developed for helping siblings
master the basic skills they need to be playmates. It is important to remember that the ages of both children, and the degree of mental retardation (if any) shown by the child with
autism, will be important factors in determining how complex
the play becomes.

Children as Teachers

As you may know from working with your child with autism, the basic principles of behavior management are valuable educational tools. Several decades of research have helped to refine behavioral procedures into highly sophisticated methods for creating an effective learning environment. The use of rewards (positive reinforcement), well-delivered instructions, and physical and verbal guidance (prompts) are among the tried and true methods for helping children with autism learn.

Research also tells us that consistency of teaching methods and expectations for behavior across settings and across people is very important to help children with autism learn. These children do their best when there is a high degree of consistency in other people's expectations for them. If a teacher is rewarding a child with praise and favorite toys for attempts to communicate, and his parents do not know that they should do the same, he will have a hard time learning to use his speech at home.

It was not long after professionals began to use behavioral techniques that they realized parents would have to become partners in their child's education to ensure consistency from school to home (Lovaas, Koegel, Simmons, & Long, 1973). Failing to involve parents often means that children with autism will not transfer their skills from school to home and community. The importance of training parents in behavioral skills has become a fundamental assumption in the treatment of children with autism. It is clear that parents who provide a consistent home learning environment for their child can make an important contribution to that child's development (Harris, 1983).

Given the valuable role of parents as teachers, it is not surprising that some people have wondered whether siblings could learn and apply behavioral teaching skills. The answer to that question is, yes, children can learn to use basic behavioral skills just as adults do (e.g., Colletti & Harris, 1977). However, that is not a very informative answer, because the question is really more complicated. To be fair to children, we need to ask what their "teaching" responsibilities for their sibling should be based on their age. Maturity becomes an important factor here. What we expect from an 8–year-old would differ sharply from what we expect from a 15–year-old, and our expectations for both children would differ from those for an adult.

Is it appropriate for siblings, especially when they are young, to become teachers for their brother or sister with autism? Should they be expected to spend an hour or two a day interacting with the child with autism? You may have concerns about imposing too many demands on your children. You might argue that children must be permitted to be children, and not take on the obligations of parents or teachers. I share those concerns. I agree that children are not adults and should not have an adult's responsibilities. If we agree on that point, it then raises the next question. If children should not be burdened with the task of helping a brother or sister with autism learn to control disruptive behavior, master self-help skills, speech, or academic materials, is there still a meaningful role for them to play in relation to their brother or sister? I believe there is.

For older siblings, those who are preadolescents or adolescents, psychologist Bruce Baker (1989) offers an interesting approach to sibling training. Baker teaches these siblings basic information about their brother's or sister's disability, encourages group sharing of experiences, and offers the young people exposure to basic behavioral skills. However, he does not press the siblings to take on teaching responsibilities toward their brother or sister with mental retardation. Baker reports that children who completed his training program spent more time with their mentally retarded sibling than they had before training and that the quality of their interactions was improved. Thus, for older children, a modified "sibling as teacher" role may be useful.

Your teenager may be happy to spend a half hour a day being a tutor for his little sister. I know high-school-aged youngsters who take an active and creative role in teaching their brother or sister with autism meaningful life skills. For example, one adolescent taught her 13–year-old sister how to pick out clothes that went together in color and pattern. Another young man decided to teach his brother with autism how to shoot a basketball, and took on the activity as a personal, and pleasurable project. In both of these cases the initiation came from the teenagers, and not from their parents.

The approach taken by Baker (1989) may not be appropriate for younger children. There is a better approach for these youngsters. The work that David Celiberti and I did with young siblings of children with autism grew out of our desire to help both the child with autism and the normally developing sibling become more fully siblings (Celiberti & Harris, 1993). We did not want to place the normally developing child in the role of an auxiliary parent. To accomplish our goal, we focused on one of the most fundamental activities of childhood, play. We wondered whether young siblings of children with autism could use simple behavioral skills to engage their brother or sister in play. As we saw in the case of Nick and Rhona Laurel that opened this chapter, such learning is not only possible, it is often enjoyable for both children.

Teaching Play Skills

Psychologist David Celiberti has done extensive research developing methods to teach young children the skills they need to play with a brother or sister with autism (Celiberti, 1993, Celiberti & Harris, 1993). In his early work Celiberti worked directly with the siblings, teaching them behavioral skills such as how to praise good play and how to initiate new games. More recently, he shifted his focus to teaching parents how to teach their children these same skills. This approach keeps the focus on the family. His work shows that parents can be good teachers of behavioral skills. At least as important, he found that the children enjoy playing together. In his research Celiberti showed parents how to teach skills to their children and then measured the changes in how the children played. Celiberti found that the children became more skillful playmates and that they enjoyed being with their brother or sister with autism more after training than they had before.

In teaching children how to be playmates, Celiberti found it was important that the normally developing child want to learn the skills, and not be pressured into doing so. He talked privately with each sibling before training to be certain it was something the child wanted to do. A few children decided they did not want to be part of the project. You will need to make that kind of assessment of your child's motivation. You should not pressure a reluctant brother or sister to learn these skills. Instead, explore why your child is hesitant and try to solve those problems. For example, your child may resent the time demands, be afraid of his sister, be concerned that he will not be able to learn the skills, or have angry or jealous feelings. You should only do this training if your child seems interested, and you should stop when he wants to stop.

Before you can teach your children how to play together, you yourself need to understand the basics of behavioral teaching. Quite simply—you can't teach what you don't know! The skills you should know include how to give clear, simple instructions, how to reward good behavior, and how to give help when your child needs a prompt in order to respond. There are good books you can read if you want to refresh your memory on training you received some years ago. For example, *Teaching Developmentally Disabled Children* (Lovaas, 1981) and *Steps to Independence* (Baker & Brightman, 1989) are both books parents tell me are helpful to them. You may hear different names for these behavioral techniques including behavior modification or applied behavior analysis, but these terms all refer to essentially the same methods of teaching.

If you have not had any training in behavioral skills, you may want to seek some parent training before you try to teach these skills to your children. The brief overview I am giving in this chapter will be helpful if you understand the behavioral basics, but it is not enough to make you skillful in behavioral methods if you do not already understand the essentials of these procedures. Incidentally, if you have never had any parent training you will find it useful for many purposes and should do your best to obtain training from a competent person. A psychologist skilled in behavior modification or an educator experienced in working with people with autism are the people who usually do this kind of training. Your child's school or the local autism society chapter may help you find such a person.

In order to teach your normally developing child to become an effective teacher/playmate for his brother or sister with autism, you should follow a series of three steps. First, remember to go slowly, do just a little each day, and be liberal in your praise of your children and your pride in yourself. Second, create the setting for teaching. Third, teach three basic skills:

    a) giving instructions
    b) rewarding good behavior
    c) prompting new skills.

Setting the Stage

Before you start to teach, you should set the stage for play between your children. One way to do this is to select toys that are colorful, attractive, and of potential interest to both children. Toys that encourage interaction like soft balls that can be thrown or rolled between two children, trucks or cars, dollhouses, toy airports, garages, and doctor kits are all toys that lend themselves to joint play. By contrast, crayons, scissors, and books lend themselves more readily to separate, parallel play that does not require much interaction. For the teaching sessions you are creating, choose toys that are likely to encourage interactions between your children.

In the beginning it is a good idea to select activities that your child with autism already understands. If you are not certain that she knows how to play with a particular toy, find that out in a play session of your own. As we saw in the case of Rhona Laurel and Nick that opened this chapter, if the child with autism knows how to manipulate the toys, that makes it easier for the sibling-teacher to master the teaching skills. Later, she may decide to teach her brother new activities, but at first she should stick to things where she has a high chance of success.

Not only should the toys encourage interaction, they should also be age appropriate. Select toys and activities with an eye toward the developmental level of both children. The games should not exceed either child's skill level. For example, an older sister can create a "let's pretend" routine which involves the child with autism. She might use a doll and some plastic food items to play house and assign her younger brother the role of feeding the doll. If that is too complicated, she can push cars or roll a ball with him. Similarly, if your normally developing child is six years old or younger, pretend play may be more difficult for her to manage, and the children may engage in more concrete play together such as rolling balls, pushing cars, doing puzzles, and so forth. Keep in mind also the intellectual level of your child with autism. If she has normal intelligence, she will be able to master more complex skills than if she has mental retardation. The child with mental retardation will have trouble with the rules needed to play some games, and with concepts such as sorting by color or number that may be essential to some activities. Your child's fine motor abilities should also be considered and materials selected that can be readily manipulated.

Your 13–year-old child with autism is too old for the kinds of play I just described. The focus for a child this age could be on playing video games, ball games, or learning the latest teenage dances. Adolescents can learn to use exercise equipment, to jog, or go bowling. Although I am presenting the material in this chapter in relation to younger children, the same behavioral techniques can be applied to these older, teenage-appropriate activities. However, if your normally developing child is much younger than the child with autism, the activities will have to be simple enough for the younger child. It is better that an activity be too easy than too hard. Your child's teacher probably has a wealth of information about appropriate games and activities and may even be able to tell you where to shop for materials.

Initially you should schedule brief play times, perhaps 10 or 15 minutes once or twice each day. You should be present during these sessions because they are designed for teaching, and not yet for independent play. Later, as your children enjoy playing together, they will spontaneously seek one another out, and may play for longer periods. However, as your child is first learning how to play with his brother or sister with autism, the experience may not be very rewarding and should be brief to maintain the interest of both children.

To teach your child the specific skills he will need, you should first model the behavior yourself. For example, if you are teaching your son how to get his sister's attention, start the lesson by sitting down with your daughter among the toys and showing him how you make sure she is physically oriented toward you and looking at you when you give a direction. After demonstrating this for a few minutes as part of your play interaction with your daughter, give your son a chance to practice the skill and praise him liberally for his attempts to do as you suggested.

As you coach from the sidelines, give lots of positive feedback and gentle suggestions for improvement. For example, you might say, "That was great the way you got Donna to look at you. Don't forget to be sure she is turned toward you when

TABLE 1
Giving Effective Commands
1. Put the man in the truck.
2. Throw me the ball.
3. Make the cow say moo.
4. Push the car into the garage.
5. Give me the doll.
6. Give the doll her bottle.
7. Make sounds like a pussy cat.
8. Help me move the chair.
9. Put your hands on top of the drum.
10. Blow bubbles.

you talk to her." Often it is the praise of the adult teacher which sustains the sibling during the process of learning these basic skills because the child with autism may still be quite unresponsive and not much fun as a playmate (Celiberti, 1993). So, be generous and specific in your praise. Tell your son what he did that pleases you and say it in a way that conveys your pleasure.

Each time you model good teaching skills for your child you will include all of the components of good teaching, but your focus will be one skill at a time. If you are teaching your son to give good directions, be sure to emphasize this skill, even though you will also be rewarding his sister for her responses to your directions. Shine the spotlight on one thing at a time. When he masters the first skill, move on to the next. He may begin to learn some of the other skills just from watching you, but keep your own focus on one activity.

One important word of caution: young children should not be expected to deal with a sibling's tantrums, aggressive behavior, or other disruptive acts. Be prepared to intervene if these occur. It is important that your child feel safe in the play sessions. Some children with autism may go through a flurry of disruptive behavior while their brother or sister is first learning how to be a good teacher/playmate. Be sure you keep these behaviors under good control.

Giving Clear Instructions

Being a good teacher involves knowing how to give instructions. These directions should be clear and simple. They should also be given at a slow enough pace for the child with autism to respond. The sibling-teacher should learn that it is important to avoid repeating himself, giving the same command again and again. He should ask his sister to do something, and if she does not begin to comply within 5 seconds, he should give her a physical or verbal prompt to do so. He should not just repeat the command. This kind of "nagging" usually does not do much good. In fact, it often teaches a child to ignore directions rather than to follow them. For example, if a brother asks his sister to "Make the sound of a cow," and she does not respond, he should say "moo" softly and praise her when she imitates him.

The first step to teach your son in giving an instruction is to make sure he has his sister's attention. She should be looking at her brother or focused on the play materials when he gives the instruction. A child who is not paying attention is not likely to follow directions.

Instructions, especially for children with autism, should be clear and uncomplicated. Table 1 gives examples of good instructions that are clear and easy to follow. Avoid complicated, multiple commands like, "Put it over there and then get another one and bring it to me." A better way to give those same instructions would be to say, "Put the car on the floor." Then wait for her to do so; when she does, say "Get a car from the garage." When she does, say "Bring me the car." The simple and specific language in these instructions and the slow pacing makes it more likely that a child can comply. For a child with more language and a better memory, commands can be combined. For example, your son could say, "Get the car from the garage and push it to me."

If your son has difficulty learning how to give effective instructions, spend some separate time with him playing the game of "Tell Me What to Do." In this game, which is a kind of "Simon Says," first you give him an instruction and then he gives you one. You can give each other clear, but sometimes silly, directions to make this learning fun. For example, "put the bowl on your head" or "put the glove on your foot." As you play, give him feedback on his instructions, praising him for being clear and specific. For example, say "Great job, you told me exactly what to do," or "You told me right where to put the car. You really know how to give good directions."

Being Rewarding

One of the essentials of being a good teacher is providing enthusiastic praise and affection for the student. Kids can do a terrific job of this! In teaching your child how to play with a brother or sister who has autism, your child must learn how to reward good play behaviors with specific praise. Saying things like, "Great throwing the ball to me," or "I like the way

you put the doll in the carriage" are examples of verbal rewards that both praise and specify the desired behavior. Your
child should learn to do this with energy and clarity.

If necessary, your child's praise of her sibling with autism
can also be accompanied by small treats like pieces of cookie
or pretzel. However, the play itself is intended as the most important reward, and if food is not essential to learning, you
need not use it. Instead, your son might pat his sister on the
back, or give her a tickle or a hug from time to time. Teach
your child to give the praise and other rewards immediately after his sister follows his instructions. If he does use food as a
reward, you should also teach him to use praise each time he
offers food.

After the children have played together for a while, you
can provide a very natural food reward in the form of milk and
cookies, or chips and juice, at the end of their session. This is
a reward for both children.

One useful teaching activity to do with your child is to
help him make up a list of many reinforcing things he can say
to his sister (Celiberti, 1993). This should be done at a separate time from the play sessions. See Table 2 for some examples of rewarding statements. Help your child think of
examples he can use with his own sister. Do not forget to reward your son as he does this. You can praise him for his crea-
tivity in thinking of so many good sentences and let him know
how much you appreciate his effort. Another fun way to teach
him to be rewarding is to play a game in which he reinforces
you with a penny each time you make a correct response, and
you in turn give him a penny for each effective rewarding
statement he makes to you. Older children may not need

TABLE 2
Being Rewarding

1. Great job throwing me the ball.
2. I like how you are feeding the doll.
3. You're great at saying moo.
4. Wow, what big bubbles!
5. When you bark you sound just like a puppy. Good work!
6. That is really a big tower. Great building!
7. Nice throw, Tom. You threw that really hard.
8. Good talking. You sound just like the airplane pilot.
9. I really like it when you play trucks with me.

these games, but will rely more on observing your model and getting feedback from you on their performance.

Giving Help

When a child does not understand how to do something, we may give him physical or verbal assistance (technically called prompts) to follow the direction. For example, if a girl wanted to teach her brother with autism how to roll a toy car into a garage she might say, "Jack, put the car in the garage." She would give him five seconds to follow her instruction, and if Jack did not do so, she would take his hand, put it on the car, and push the car into the garage, saying, "Good, you put the car in the garage." Putting her hand over Jack's to guide the car is an example of a physical prompt.

It is important that children with autism not become too dependent on physical prompts, so we always make sure to give the child time to respond on his own (usually 5 seconds), and then we provide no more prompt than is absolutely essential. Gradually we fade the prompt until it is no longer required. For example, in this case the sister might make her touch softer, and then shift to just pointing at the garage, and finally fade the prompt entirely. However, if her brother began to make a mistake, for example turning over the truck to spin the wheels, she would not wait 5 seconds to prompt him, but would immediately provide the guidance he needed to respond correctly. Prompting can be a hard skill to learn. You should practice it with your child until he understands both when to prompt and how to decrease his prompt. This can be done with a combination of modeling by you and feedback to your child as she practices either in a rehearsal with you or a play session with her brother.

If your child with autism does not like to be touched, his sister should not be expected to use these prompts. Rather, the first step would be to teach the child to accept this kind of contact from you, and then to introduce the sibling's touch. Your child's teacher, the school psychologist, or a physical therapist may have suggestions about how to increase your child's tolerance of touch.

Finishing Touches

After your child has mastered how to deliver instructions, reward good behavior, and provide physical or verbal guidance, there is one more useful skill you can teach her. This involves rewarding spontaneous play behavior when it occurs. So far this chapter has focused on teaching the child with autism to follow instructions. However, it is even more fun when he initiates the play himself. Your daughter should become alert to these spontaneous events and reward them with as much energy as possible. If she has taught her brother how to play catch with the big round ball and one day he picks up a football to throw to her, she should praise him with great energy. Similarly, if they have been playing with toy trucks and he picks up a toy airplane, she should respond with enthusiasm to his initiation. The same would hold true for new language. If her brother uses a new word, she should express her delight. However, this does not mean she is always obligated to play with him, although ideally she would respond with warmth even when she turns him down. She can refuse when she wants to play alone, study, or be with a friend. Parents should help the child with autism accept these realistic limits.

With Very Young Children

In working with families who have preschool children, I suggest that family games be developed which involve the child with autism and the sibling. This may help to make the children's interactions more fun. An example is a game of "Come Here," which involves calling a child's name: "Zachery, come here." When the child does come, he is swept into the arms of an adult for a tickle, toss in the air, etc. The command may initially be given from only a few feet away, and the child with autism gently propelled toward the adult. Gradually the distance is increased, and parents may call from different rooms of the house, while partially hidden, and so forth. Normally developing preschoolers can enjoy the game, and for the child with autism it is valuable learning about following instructions. Similarly, a game of "Do This" in which nonverbal imitation is rewarded with hugs and applause can be a pleasure for both children. This imitation can be gradually expanded into that childhood favorite of "Simon Says."

Closing Comments

Playing together is one of the important experiences that brothers and sisters share. It is part of building the sibling bond. When one sibling has autism that play is often disrupted by the difficult-to-manage behaviors and lack of apparent response by the child with autism. Research suggests that siblings can learn how to help their brother or sister become a playmate. A sibling who can master the basics of giving effective commands, providing generous rewards for correct responses, and offering necessary physical or verbal guidance may find that these skills change difficult interactions into pleasurable ones. A parent who is skillful in the basics of behavioral teaching can help a sibling master these skills. However, it is very important that the sibling be motivated to learn the skills and that playtime not become a burden for her.

PARENTS SPEAK

Over the years, some of the strategies I have used to develop the relationship between Matt, who has autism, and his sister Annie have revolved around play. Activities that involve music and song have been particularly effective—for example, "Row Row Row Your Boat," "Ring Around the Rosie," "If You're Happy and You Know it," and "Wheels on the Bus." I have also taught Matt and Annie how to dance together.

Matt has always loved playing chase games, especially being surprised. I took it a step further, and taught them how to play "Hide and Seek." Matt has also learned how to direct Annie in a chase game through different rooms in the house. He chooses the path she'll take to run and surprise him (i.e., "Annie come chase me. Go through the living room."). In addition, I utilized this idea of chase for pretend play as well, for example, "playing monster."

Finally, my children have benefitted from some more sedentary activities, such as coloring, playing with "Play Doh," and reading. When the children were younger, I naturally did the reading. Now that Annie is learning to read, she loves to read to Matt, and he is encouraged to do the same.

My daughter leaned how to go about getting eye contact and the value of reinforcement. The important thing about the play program is that it was designed for her and other siblings. She now has the basic skills necessary to successfully have fun with her brother. These skills could be carried over to all settings. My daughter was important to her brother's life—she could help him, play with him, laugh with him. What a boost to her self-esteem and family harmony.

When you sent home a letter to my mom asking her about siblings, I asked her if I could write to you. She said sure, so here it is. I want you to know how great it is to play with Art. Sometimes I still get mad at him. But I like it when he learns to throw the ball with me and roll cars. Next, I'm going to teach him to pretend to be an animal like a dog or cat or lion.

When I first started to get my kids to play together, I wondered if it was more work than it was worth. Eric, my boy with autism, can be a tough cookie, and he could really give my daughter, Sarah, a hard time. For a long time I pretty much had to sit there and watch so I could pick Eric up and put him in time out if he got rowdy. But, gradually he started to enjoy being with Sarah, and now it is rare that he gets out of control. When he does, Sarah knows to call me and I put him in time out. It took three or four months to get it rolling, but now it works pretty well.

References

Alessandri, M. (1992). *The influence of sex-role orientation on the marital adjustment and degree of parental involvement in family work: A comparison of mothers and fathers of children with autism and mothers and fathers of normally developing children.* Unpublished doctoral dissertation, Rutgers, The State University of New Jersey, Piscataway NJ.

August, G. J., Stewart, M. A., & Tsai, L. (1981). The incidence of cognitive disabilities in the siblings of autistic children. *British Journal of Psychiatry, 138*, 416-422.

Baker, B. L. (1989). *Parent training and developmental disabilities.* Washington, DC: American Association on Mental Retardation.

Baker, B. L. & Brightman, A. J. (1989). *Steps to independence.* Baltimore, MD: Paul H. Brookes.

Bank, S.P. & Kahn, M. D. (1982). *The sibling bond.* New York: Basic Books.

Bartak, L., Rutter, M., & Cox, A. (1975). A comparative study of infantile autism and specific developmental language disorder. I. The children. *British Journal of Psychiatry, 126*, 127-145.

Boer, F., Goedhart, A. W., & Treffers, P. D. A. (1992). Siblings and their parents. In F. Boer & J. Dunn (Eds.), *Children's sibling relationships. Developmental and clinical issues* (pp. 41-54). Hillsdale, NJ: Erlbaum Associates.

Brodzinsky, D. & Schechter, M. (Eds.) (1990). *The psychology of adoption.* New York: Oxford University Press.

Buhrmester, D. (1992). The developmental courses of sibling and peer relationships. In F. Boer & J. Dunn (Eds.), *Children's sibling relationships. Developmental and clinical issues* (pp. 19-40). Hillsdale, NJ: Erlbaum Associates.

Celiberti, D. A. (1993). *Training parents of children with autism to promote sibling play: Randomized trials of three alternative training interventions*. Unpublished doctoral dissertation. Rutgers, The State University of New Jersey, Piscataway, NJ.

Celiberti, D. A. & Harris, S. L. (1993). The effects of a play skills intervention for siblings of children with autism. *Behavior Therapy, 24*, 573-599.

Colletti, G. & Harris, S. L. (1977). Behavior modification in the home: Siblings as behavior modifiers, parents as observers. *Journal of Abnormal Child Psychology, 1*, 21-30.

Dunn, J. (1992). Sisters and brothers: Current issues in developmental research. In F. Boer & J. Dunn (Eds.), *Children's sibling relationships. Developmental and clinical issues* (pp. 1-17). Hillsdale, NJ: Erlbaum Associates.

Folstein, S. E. & Rutter, M. L. (1987). Autism. Familial aggregation and genetic implications. In E. Schopler & G. B. Mesibov (Eds.), *Neurobiological issues in autism* (pp. 83-105). New York: Plenum.

Forgatch, M. & Patterson, G. (1989). *Parents and adolescents living together. Part 2: Family problem solving*. Eugene, OR: Castalia Publishing Co.

Harris, S. L. (1983). *Families of the developmentally disabled: A guide to behavioral intervention*. Elmsford, NY: Pergamon Press.

Harris, S. L., Handleman, J. S., & Palmer, C. (1985). Parents and grandparents view the autistic child. *Journal of Autism and Developmental Disorders, 15,* 127-137.

Holmes, N. & Carr, J. (1991). The pattern of care in families of adults with a mental handicap: A comparison between families of autistic adults and Down syndrome adults. *Journal of Autism and Developmental Disorders, 21,* 159-176.

Jenkins, J. (1992). Sibling relationships in disharmonious homes: Potential difficulties and protective effects. In F. Boer & J. Dunn (Eds.), *Children's sibling relationships. Developmental and clinical issues* (pp. 125-138). Hillsdale, NJ: Erlbaum Associates.

Lobato, D. (1990). *Brothers, sisters and special needs.* Baltimore, MD: Paul H. Brookes.

Lovaas, O. I. (1981). *Teaching developmentally disabled children: The me book.* Baltimore, MD: University Park Press.

Lovaas, O. I., Koegel, R., Simmons, J. D., & Long, J. S. (1973). Some generalization and follow-up measures on autistic children in behavior therapy. *Journal of Applied Behavior Analysis, 6,* 131-166.

McHale, S. M. & Harris, V. S. (1992). Children's experiences with disabled and nondisabled siblings: Links with personal adjustment and relationship evaluations. In F. Boer & J. Dunn (Eds.), *Children's siblings relationships. Developmental and clinical issues* (pp. 83-100). Hillsdale, NJ: Erlbaum Associates.

McHale, S. M., Sloan, J., & Simeonsson, R. J. (1986). Sibling relationships of children with autistic, mentally retarded, and nonhandicapped brothers and sisters. *Journal of Autism and Developmental Disorders, 16,* 399-413.

Powers, M. D. (Ed.) (1989). *Children with autism: A parents' guide*. Rockville, MD: Woodbine House.

Ritvo, E. R., Freeman, B. J., Mason-Brothers, A., Mo, A., & Ritvo, A. M. (1985). Concordance for the syndrome of autism in 40 pairs of afflicted twins. *American Journal of Psychiatry, 142*, 74-77.

Rodrigue, J. R., Geffken, G. R., & Morgan, S. B. (1993). Perceived competence and behavioral adjustment of siblings of children with autism. *Journal of Autism and Developmental Disorders, 23*, 665-674.

Rutter, M. (1985). Infantile autism and other pervasive developmental disorders. In M. Rutter & L. Herzov (Eds.), *Child and adolescent psychiatry: Modern approaches*, (pp. 545-566). London: Blackwell.

Seligman, M. & Darling, R. B. (1989). *Ordinary families, special children: A systems approach to childhood disability*. New York: Guilford Press.

Index

About the author

Sandra L. Harris, Ph.D. is Professor and Dean at the Graduate School of Applied and Professional Psychology at Rutgers University in New Jersey. She is also Executive Director of the Douglass Developmental Disabilities Center, a Rutgers-based program for children and adolescents with autism, which she founded in 1972.